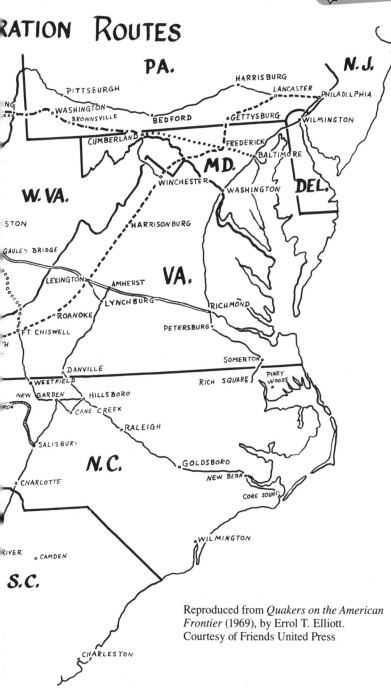

ᴿATION ROUTES

PA.

N. J.

HARRISBURG

PITTSBURGH
LANCASTER
PHILADELPHIA

NG
xxx
WASHINGTON
BROWNSVILLE
BEDFORD
GETTYSBURG
WILMINGTON

CUMBERLAND
FREDERICK
BALTIMORE

MD.
WINCHESTER
WASHINGTON
DEL.

W. VA.

STON
HARRISONBURG

GAULEY BRIDGE

VA.

LEXINGTON
AMHERST
LYNCHBURG
RICHMOND

ROANOKE
PETERSBURG

FT. CHISWELL

H

SOMERTON

DANVILLE
RICH SQUARE
PINEY WOODS

WESTFIELD

NEW GARDEN
HILLSBORO

RD
CANE CREEK
RALEIGH

SALISBURY

N.C.

GOLDSBORO

CHARLOTTE
NEW BERN

CORE SOUND

WILMINGTON

RIVER
CAMDEN

S.C.

Reproduced from *Quakers on the American
Frontier* (1969), by Errol T. Elliott.
Courtesy of Friends United Press

CHARLESTON

OUR QUAKER ANCESTORS

Finding Them in Quaker Records

Ellen Thomas Berry, M.A., C.G.
David Allen Berry, B.A., C.G.

Baltimore
GENEALOGICAL PUBLISHING CO., INC.
1987

Library of Congress Catalogue Card Number 87-80356
International Standard Book Number 0-8063-1190-8
Made in the United States of America

For Jason and Julie

CONTENTS

Appendices

PREFACE

A number of years ago we began researching a family line whose members, according to family tradition, were Quakers. Even though those living at the time did not belong to The Religious Society of Friends, the story persisted. After diligent work in the State Library of Pennsylvania, where no trace of the family in question could be found, we traveled to Berks County where we knew some of the family had lived during the first half of the nineteenth century. There we uncovered the Quaker background and, in fact, found that all family lines were Friends when they immigrated to the Welsh Tract of Chester County, Pennsylvania in the 1680s. However, this discovery was more the result of good fortune than knowledge of how to use Quaker records. This knowledge was to come later after we found that Quaker genealogy, a subject in its own right, demands special research methods.

The discovery of a Quaker history in the family has led us into the most interesting research we have encountered in our genealogical pursuits. Out of this work in which we have been involved during the past twelve years, came the realization that a guidebook for those just beginning Quaker genealogy could save others the many hours we have spent acquiring the rudimentary knowledge needed to find our way through these records.

Records of The Religious Society of Friends are comprehensive, but they are difficult—in fact, often impossible—to use the first time you attempt a search. The fact that you can be almost certain that the name you seek is somewhere in the maze is little comfort when you lack the key to finding and interpreting the records.

We hope this book will provide that key. It is not meant as a reference work for experienced Quaker historians. Rather, it is designed specifically to give some idea of the kinds of material preserved by The Religious Society of Friends; to describe the locations of at least some of these records; and to help guide the researcher through the maze of those records.

We have included an Appendix which we hope will be informative and helpful. A list of terms unique to Quakers will start you down a fascinating trail, searching for ancestors who were Friends. The Bibliography contains a very small portion of the printed material available in the form of histories of Quaker families as well as transcribed birth, death, marriage, and membership records. Because rules of the Friends against marrying outside meeting lowered the already-small number of eligible candidates, a well-researched genealogy may well contain the name for which you are searching.

The research methods and the suggestions for locating the records are intended primarily for the years up to 1850. After this time, vast changes due to separations within the organization may complicate research. Although record-keeping methods remained virtually the same, in order to locate the records you may need to know to what branch of the Society your ancestor belonged. The yearly meetings listed in Appendix G have a code letter designating their present-day affiliations.

If there are errors, we take full responsibility. We have endeavored to be as accurate as possible under circumstances where each repository is autonomous. The method we have described for determining the monthly meeting to which an ancestor belonged is our own. We hope it works for you as it has for us.

As in any project, many people have been involved. We

would like to thank each of them, but particularly our thanks go to the staffs of the libraries at Friends Historical Library, Swarthmore, Pennsylvania; at the Quaker Collection, Haverford College, Haverford, Pennsylvania; at the Quaker Collection, Guilford College, Greensboro, North Carolina; at the Quaker Collection, Wilmington College, Wilmington, Ohio; and at the Quaker Collection, Malone College, Canton, Ohio. We also are indebted to Elizabeth H. Moger, Keeper of the Records at Haviland Records Room in New York City, for her assistance. She has very graciously consented to our using portions of her excellent article published by the Central New York Genealogical Society in its publication *Tree Talks,* Vol. 25, No. 1 (March 1985). The article is based on a talk Mrs. Moger gave to the Society in 1984. And to Harvey G. Shulman and James Edgar we offer our thanks for invaluable technical assistance.

Ellen Thomas Berry, M.A., C.G.
David Allen Berry, B.A., C.G.

Columbus, Ohio
1 October 1986

CHAPTER I

INTRODUCTION

The Religious Society of Friends, or Quakers, has a rich storehouse of records kept from its beginning in the mid-1600s to the present. This book is designed specifically to help newcomers to Quaker genealogy first to locate the records, then to find their way through the maze of those records. It is not intended as a reference work for experienced Quaker historians. There are vast differences among Quaker records and the genealogist must know which ones to use. This book can save you a great amount of time and you will benefit from the inevitable mistakes we made as interested but uninitiated novices. The study of Quaker records is mechanically different from that of other religious organizations. More emphasis must be placed on historical context, because organizational history and record-keeping are closely related. Unless you are careful —and knowledgeable—you can become hopelessly lost and find yourself giving up on one of the richest sources of genealogical records you could ever hope to find.

Across the United States there are small towns with names which have a certain rhythm or quality of sound. As you move south and west from the Eastern Seaboard to the Mississippi River and beyond, through Virginia and the swamplands of the Carolinas to Georgia, you will see names like Radnor, Concord, Salem, New Garden, Goshen, Cedar Creek, and others which combine Biblical and geographical origins. These names are a part of one of the most interesting facets of early American history. They indicate that, at least at one time, the area was populated by The Religious Society of Friends. The Quakers were once an influential part of their communities. They moved from their early settlements in the original eastern colonies and called their new homes by familiar names, much as they had done when they arrived from England and Wales. In some of these towns you may find a rectangular building, usually stretching east to west and facing south, which may still be used as a meetinghouse. In all probability it will have the same name as the village or town.

If you were to visit any of these meetinghouses today, you might find a record of almost every event which took place at that location from the time of its establishment. These records include information on births, marriages, and deaths, but they also note the names of residents moving to and from the area and their places of origin, as well as committee actions on a wide variety of topics, including requests to individuals to leave the meeting and the reasons for the request. In addition, there would be records of announced intentions of marriage, followed by the actual wedding record naming not only the bride and groom but all those present, among whom may be found the parents, brothers, sisters, and perhaps other relatives of the newlyweds. If the old records are not at the meetinghouse itself, it is possible to determine where they have been sent and where the original records or microfilm copies can be used by the general public. In other words, you will find a genealogist's dream. There is an amazing number of these records in existence. You only need to know where they are and how to use them. That is the focus of this book.

The Society of Friends began in the same religious turmoil of seventeenth-century England which produced the Puritans. The Quakers also immigrated to America to escape severe religious persecution. Although Quakers first saw American shores during the 1650s, it was not until 1682 that large numbers started to emigrate from the British Isles and smaller numbers from continental Europe. It was in this year that William Penn landed just south of what is now Philadelphia to exercise his proprietorship of the present states of Pennsylvania and Delaware. Because of their stubbornness or strong-mindedness (depending upon how you view it), the Quakers' influence far exceeded their numbers. They were a study of contradictions. Although they espoused religious freedom, they required their own members to worship in a specified manner. No organization had more rules regarding removal from approved status than the Quakers. By today's standards these rules seem trivial and even arrogant. It now seems ironic that it was precisely this dictatorial image that the Society wanted to avoid at all costs. They were truly "plain people," but at the same time they were shrewd merchants. Their honesty in personal and business dealings was renowned. Their treatment of the Indians is a classic study in how other white Americans should have conducted themselves. However, even in this area they were not completely faultless. They abhorred slavery, but some families owned slaves. They were against war of any kind, but still some fought in the Revolutionary and Civil Wars.

The Quakers were a more mobile society than most religious groups which came to early America. Whether their travels through the South to the Midwest were prompted by religious fervor, the clash of political and religious beliefs (e.g. slavery), or simply the desire for land and opportunities is now a moot point. The fact is they did move in large numbers, and in doing so left a trail of records unsurpassed by any other religious organization.

There is another side to this story. The same doctrine which required record-keeping also forbade religious rituals and any form of self-aggrandizement. In the early years even grave markers were prohibited, as were personal histories (although some histories do exist, particularly of people prominent in the movement). Therefore, it is often difficult for a genealogist to place an ancestor in the proper historical perspective. However, the voluminous records more than make up for these deficiencies. It is always safe to say that anyone interested in tracing ancestors is indeed fortunate if a connection can be made with Quakers, for it means there is a good chance that comprehensive primary records can be found.

In our travels throughout Pennsylvania, Maryland, Virginia, and North and South Carolina, and in conversations with Quaker librarians, it became apparent that research in Quaker genealogy would be greatly facilitated by a definitive handbook describing the differences that exist between Friends' records and denominational church records; in particular, we hoped to delineate the methods necessary to locate and interpret data critical to genealogists.

Before there can be any clear understanding of Quaker records, one must know something of the history of The Religious Society of Friends. There was no question of whether or not to keep records; it was a dictate from the Society's founder, George Fox, that records be kept. This idea is so foreign to modern denominational church practices that some introduction to Quakerism is necessary, and the next chapter is intended to fulfill this need.

CHAPTER II

BACKGROUND AND HISTORY
OF THE RELIGIOUS SOCIETY OF FRIENDS

The history of a particular religious denomination or sect would not ordinarily be included in a book devoted to procedures for locating that denomination's extant records. However, some knowledge of Quaker history is not only useful, but it will help you obtain maximum benefit from the records.

Since the Quaker movement and the rise of Puritanism occurred about the same time, it has been a common belief that they were affiliated, or even had the same basic doctrines. Yet there was no theological or ideological relationship between Quakerism and Puritanism other than the fact that both arose from the obsession of many members of English society to free themselves from the tyranny of the State Church. Each movement followed its own path, as did many other sects which sprang up in England at the same general time but have long since passed from the contemporary religious scene.

The Quaker movement was the work of a single person, George Fox (1624-1691). As a very young boy, Fox was puzzled by the selfish attitudes of the very men who were entrusted with the progress and well-being of the population. These men, usually associated with the Church of England and closely connected to the Crown, were grasping, avaricious citizens, powerful and invariably wealthy. Their chief concern was the furthering of their personal interests. George Fox could not reconcile the actions and deeds of these men with their talk. Along with many others, Fox was eventually to suffer terrible persecution from these men, who operated under the sanctions of the Church of England.

George Fox was seeking an inner peace he could not find in the English religious and educational institutions of his time. Early in life he reached certain conclusions which greatly affected his future organization. In 1652 he began to preach that "Christ speaks directly to each human soul who seeks Him; spiritual life depends upon direct communion with Him; all men may find salvation and life in Him."[1] Fox had concluded that religion was a matter of the spirit, not of the intellect. He devised the concept of the "Inner Light," a force latent in all men which ultimately guides the faith and actions of individuals. This idea is the heart of Quakerism. No longer were paid leaders needed for guidance. Each person could be his own "minister or priest" with the presence of this "Inner Light." With the preaching of this concept, George Fox was flying directly in the face of the Church of England and signing his own arrest warrant many times over. Needless to say, such a concept caught on quickly in a country as torn with strife as England in the 1600s, where the general population was hungry for any teaching which brought hope into their dreary lives. Religion and government were almost indistinguishable, and the ordinary man had very few personal freedoms or opportunities.

George Fox preached the beginnings of Quakerism in England in Leicestershire in 1644. The movement spread northward to Warwickshire (1645), Nottinghamshire (1646), and Derbyshire (1647), reaching Yorkshire in 1651. The concept of the "Inner Light" gained adherents so rapidly that by 1654 Quakers not only lived in most of the English counties (and the City of London), but also in Scotland, Ireland, and, in 1656, in America.

Fox was an energetic and zealous missionary for the fledgling movement, traveling over England and Wales, to Holland, down to the West Indies, and finally to North America. It is interesting that the first Quakers in America were two women, Ann Austin and Mary Fisher, both arriving in Boston from Barbados in 1656. They were imprisoned and returned to their point of origin. Soon, laws were passed forbidding ships' captains to bring Quakers to the shores of America. In New England, Puritan law was harsh. In 1657 a law was passed allowing an ear to be cut off any Quakers who returned to a community from which they had been expelled. The second offense resulted in the loss of the other ear, and Quakers who dared to return a third time lost their tongues.

Friends were confronted constantly with terrible persecution in Great Britain, on the Continent, and in America. The actions taken in the British Isles can be rationalized by conceding the fact that the Quakers were active and vocal about the church-state arrangement prevalent at the time. The American Puritans had no logical reasons. They arbitrarily decided that Quakers worshipped the Devil and denied authority. Their constant refusals to bow to officials, to use titles of address, and to take oaths were interpreted as signs of arrogance and iconoclasm when, ironically, the reverse was true. This is not to say that early Quakers did not have characteristics which, in many instances, made them thoroughly unlikeable to the general population. They were stubborn and obtuse about their religion and were often shrewd and wealthy businessmen. The equality of women has always been a part of the Quaker creed, even though women had their own monthly meetings within the jurisdiction of the general monthly meeting. Stephen Weeks states in his book, *Southern Quakers and Slavery,* "No Church since the days of the Apostles has allowed such great freedom in the Gospel to women as has been allowed by Friends. Under their system man and woman are equal, and Quaker women have repaid this greater liberty with an unsurpassed zeal and devotion."[2] This statement was made as an introductory remark concerning the establishment of the Quaker movement in Virginia in 1656 by Elizabeth Harris, a native of London. The first two American colonies in which Quakerism was preached,

Massachusetts and Virginia, both permitted women as principals.

It is generally believed that William Penn was one of the founders of Quakerism; however, it was not until 1666 that Penn was "convinced" and became an ardent adherent. As mentioned earlier, Quakers were in New England and parts of the South several decades before William Penn's settlement in Pennsylvania. However, his colony provided a refuge from English persecutions for the largest contingent of Quakers in America. William Penn has earned a special place in the Quaker movement in America because of the large numbers of Friends who settled in what was to become Pennsylvania and Delaware, and who were responsible for the successful religious, political, and economic climate of those colonies.

William Penn was born in England in 1644, the son of a career naval officer who had the political acumen to serve Oliver Cromwell and afterwards still be close to the returning monarch, Charles II. Cromwell had rewarded the elder Penn for his services by giving him several estates in Ireland where he could live the remainder of his life as a gentleman—which is precisely what he did. However, the elder Penn saw promise in his son William and sent him to Oxford in 1660, where he proceeded to get expelled for his outspoken and nonconformist religious beliefs. The Penns were Anglicans, but the younger William discovered he could not accept the Church's teachings without question. He was exposed to George Fox's teachings in Ireland and was converted in 1666, much to the discomfiture of his father.

Penn spent some time in an English prison because of his beliefs, but emerged strengthened in his awareness of the need for religious liberty and the right of individuals to have an active part in worship services. He first came to America in the 1670s as one of the proprietors of New Jersey, having in mind a haven for Quakers who wished to leave England.

George Fox, too, had traveled to the New World during the 1670s, visiting Quakers in Jamaica and Barbados. He had also traveled to the American mainland, stopping in North Carolina, Virginia, Maryland, the Delaware Valley, New Jersey, and Long Island. Upon Fox's return to England, he and Penn visited Europe in 1677, meeting mostly with Germans. As a result of these travels, Fox and Penn decided the broad and fertile valleys between the Delaware and Susquehanna rivers in America best suited their purposes.

When they returned to England, William Penn approached Charles II with this thought in mind. He was able to persuade the King to give him a proprietorship for what is now Pennsylvania and Delaware, using as leverage an unpaid debt of 16,000 pounds, the result of a loan which Penn's deceased father had made to the King and his brother James, Duke of York, upon their return to power. William Penn's membership in the Quaker movement made him unpopular in Court circles, yet Charles II felt a duty to stand by Penn because of the services performed by his father. Penn knew also that the King was anxious to be rid of such a controversial subject, mainly because of their religious differences, but also because of Charles' obligation to the Penn family. The King saw in William Penn's request for a grant of land an opportunity to end the entire matter quickly, discharging his debt and getting rid of Penn at the same time. Penn was given more land than he asked for or expected. The final charter specified lands lying west of the Delaware River and between the borders of Maryland and New York—in other words, the entire area of what is now the State of Pennsylvania. Penn also requested and received access to the sea in the form of the so-called Lower Counties, the present State of Delaware.

The charter was approved in 1681, and the noble experiment began. Penn issued pamphlets while still in England and offered land for sale at the most liberal terms yet seen in the American colonies (e.g. 100 pounds for 5,000 acres, with smaller amounts of land correspondingly priced). He was completely honest in describing the land and the terms. This honesty not only paid dividends in loyalty but became one of the foundation stones of the Quaker society. As mentioned previously, Penn's honest and forthright treatment of the Indians became a model which would have served well for later non-Quaker immigrants. However, even with all his efforts to act in an exemplary way, there were still problems. For instance, he over-sold town lots in Philadelphia, and Welsh Quakers who really meant to be merchants found themselves on farms west of the Schuylkill River, far from their potential marketplaces. The fact that this Welsh Tract was destined to become a part of Philadelphia's famed "Main Line" was no solace to these early settlers, who were unable to foresee such a development.

William Penn came to his colony in October, 1682, landing near what is now New Castle, Delaware. His ship was the *Welcome,* with about 130 settlers. For family tracers with possible ancestors in early Pennsylvania-Delaware, these passengers have been well-documented.[3] More than twenty ships quickly followed Penn's, each filled with Quakers anxious to start life in a location where the choice of religion was not literally a life-or-death decision.

Pennsylvania was an immediate success, but it was not a democracy. Penn appointed himself Governor with the right to reject any and all legislation. The power of the electorate was placed in the hands of a few landholders, known mostly for their substantial holdings. It was a government of elitists whose status, in Penn's aristocratic way of thinking, made them wise and virtuous. There was a large legislative assembly below this council, but it could not initiate legislation even though, theoretically, it could accept or reject any new laws. After extensive reading about early Quakers, we have come to the conclusion that as a group they were not very likeable. They could even be obnoxious in their piety. Nevertheless, they flourished without the direct help of Penn, since he spent very few years in America. He died in England in 1718, knowing that his experiment was a success.

In the case of the Friends' movement, history is so intertwined with genealogy that it is not possible to separate them.

This is due primarily to the rules established by George Fox requiring each meeting to keep complete records. Usually all you can reasonably hope to find in church archives are birth, marriage, and death records. Unless an ancestor was a minister, a prominent individual, or a large contributor, it is unlikely any additional information will be found. This does not mean these vital statistics are not extremely valuable; they may be the only available primary records. But you do not need to know the basic organization of these denominations in order to search the records and ascertain if the contents are of genealogical value. This is not true of Quaker records, which are probably more complete than those of most denominations. Also, The Religious Society of Friends has a distinctive terminology which is used to describe disciplinary actions against members and which is pertinent to genealogical research (see Glossary).

A clear understanding of the structure of the organization is needed, as the pertinence and availability of information are functions of the type of meeting being researched, with the monthly meeting being the richest by far in genealogical data. This source of information, used correctly, can be a genealogist's dream, but the types of records are all related to the history of the early establishment of the Quaker movement. Thus, it is important for any genealogist, experienced or not, to delve into this early history, for it is here that the structure for the comprehensive nature of the records originated. It is almost as though Fox had genealogy in mind when he first established the organizational structure in 1666.

In England, persecutions and atrocities were being committed on anyone advocating or supporting the Quaker movement. As early as 1653, three epistles were written by Quaker leaders. These epistles became the foundation of the movement and are of the utmost importance to present-day genealogists, although this was hardly their purpose. The first was written by William Dewsbury, recommending that regular meetings be held on a weekly and fortnightly basis, presided over by "one or two Friends who are most grown in the power and life and the pure discerning in the Truth." [4] Dewsbury also wrote that the "disorderly" are to be disowned. The third epistle dealt with organizing for the benefit of the poor and needy. But it is the second epistle which has been of tremendous help to genealogists. [5]

This second letter went out in George Fox's name and recommended that a Friend be appointed in each meeting to keep a detailed record of all the "sufferings" which had become a constant burden for the Quakers. The epistle also addressed such problems as family loyalty, the need for financial independence through hard work, and the provision of proper burial grounds for deceased Friends. In Fox's letter, the statement of greatest genealogical importance is one which ordered that records of all births, marriages, and deaths be kept by the registrar of "sufferings." Fortunately, this order was taken seriously by the various meetings, and detailed records became a vital part of the Friends movement. Indeed, in most instances these records transcended vital statistics. Of particular importance are detailed minutes of monthly meetings, including the transfer of families from one meeting to another, formation of committees, and detailed accounts of the reasons for removing a dissenter from the members' rolls. Fortunately, many of these records still exist and are available for genealogical research. These records and their use are the principal focus of this book.

With sheer determination and the drive generally associated with zealots, George Fox personally directed the spread of Quakerism and insisted on this accurate and comprehensive record-keeping. This passion for preserving accounts was carried by Fox to America. Quaker primary records are of unparalleled excellence. The momentous decision to keep complete records of all activities has resulted in a simplification of Quaker research that is almost too good to be true. On the other hand, it is too much to hope that all these records have survived or are immediately available. Great frustration results from knowing that the needed information was recorded but that it is no longer accessible. This frustration is actually worse than believing such records never existed in the first place, but we all must face the fact that some records are not extant.

The majority of Quaker immigrants to America were Anglo-Saxon, but they also came in small numbers from European countries. All left an indelible mark behind them. Many Friends came to this country by circuitous routes. For instance, the island of Barbados in the Caribbean was a center for Quakerism during the early immigration periods, and records of great genealogical value are extant for this remote area of settlement. In fact, migration routes used by the Quakers in America constitute an important chapter of this book.

It may be assumed that any organization which sets as its goal the entrenchment of its position throughout all English-speaking countries, and even the European Continent, would require a closely-knit organization. We explained earlier how George Fox apparently anticipated this need and built the Quaker movement into an organization which permitted responsibilities from top to bottom with no single facet dominating, and which at the same time allowed for expansion. As mentioned, it is necessary to understand at least the rudimentary structure of the Society in order to derive the most benefit from the records. This is so important that in the next chapter we explain the complex divisions within the Society, and how one group serves the purposes of all.

CHAPTER III

ORGANIZATION
OF THE RELIGIOUS SOCIETY OF FRIENDS

By this time you will have noticed that it is impossible to write an abbreviated Quaker history without referring to "meetings." The Religious Society of Friends was, and still is, a highly structured organization, with each component serving its own useful purpose. Each of the component meetings is an entity within itself, with freedom to function independently of other meetings. Although all are important to Quakers, for genealogists there is a great distinction in the relative importance of the different meetings. All the meetings kept records; however, only a few are of genealogical importance. The structure resembles that of a pyramid, but only in the sense that the meeting at the top of the structure covered more area. One cannot assume that a meeting had power and control over those under it—even though, in a certain sense, it did. The functions were different, so if you attempt comparisons, you soon find that you are comparing dissimilar entities. However, it is best to begin at the top and discuss the reasons for the existence of each kind of meeting and the records generated by that meeting.

Yearly Meetings

In general, the Quakers were divided into geographical sectors, although in the early years these could cover thousands of square miles. The yearly meetings represented the top of the Quaker organization. As the name implies, it was a group which met annually, usually over a period of several days or a week. Any Friend in good standing had the right to attend these meetings and openly express opinions about matters involving the Society, but appointments were made by the quarterly meetings to assure representation from all areas covered by the yearly meeting. The yearly meetings were usually held in the cities for which they were named (e.g. Baltimore Yearly met in Baltimore), although the practice was no longer possible when the meeting took the name of a state over which it had jurisdiction, e.g. Ohio Yearly Meeting.

The first yearly meeting was held at Newport, Rhode Island in 1661. This was followed by the establishment of yearly meetings in Baltimore (1672), Virginia (1673), Philadelphia (known first as Burlington—1681), New York (1695), and North Carolina (1698).

Extensive minutes were taken at all yearly meetings and were published. However, we want to emphasize that the information in these minutes is of more value to a historian than to a genealogist. A researcher must remember the purpose of these meetings. They were held to conduct the business activities of The Religious Society of Friends. Since a broad range of topics was often discussed (e.g. slavery, temperance, etc.), it is possible to follow changes in policy, but if you are interested in family data, yearly meeting records are not the place to look. The records are available in repositories at Quaker colleges and in some libraries. You can become thoroughly engrossed in reading through these minutes, but at the end of the day you will have very little information of a genealogical nature. The minutes are rarely indexed and are difficult to use. If you are persistent, it is sometimes possible to find a death notice for a prominent individual such as a minister or an elder, but unless you have unlimited time, it is better to skip the minutes of yearly meetings.

Quarterly Meetings

The next step down in the Quaker pyramid is the quarterly meeting, which was also primarily a business meeting. The quarterly meeting was made up of representatives from the various monthly meetings which came under its jurisdiction. The quarterly acted as a clearinghouse for problems of the monthly meetings, problems which could not be resolved on a local level. If these problems were too "weighty" (a favorite word among Quakers) for the quarterly meeting to solve, they were referred to the appropriate yearly meeting.

The quarterly meetings served one function which is of extreme importance to the genealogist: they established new preparative and monthly meetings when dictated by population growth in an area. Noting the establishment or "setting up" of new meetings is critical in following the path of an ancestor. Of equal importance is noting when a meeting is "laid down," the Quaker term for the breaking up of a meeting—usually when it became too small for effective work—with the remaining members sent to the meeting nearest their homes. This was a function of the quarterlies. Quarterly minutes are difficult to search because of the general absence of indexes, as well as a dearth of older records. The availability of information depends upon the accuracy and meticulousness of the clerk who was responsible for transcribing the minutes. The type of information varies tremendously from meeting to meeting and from clerk to clerk.

The quarterly meetings also served as the center of social life for the Friends. Again, records of these meetings have more historical than genealogical value, but any information which places an ancestor in a correct historical perspective is valuable. Records of early quarterly meetings are relatively rare and, considering the lack of genealogical information contained in them, searching for them should be given low priority.

Preparative Meetings
(often called Particular Meetings)

Although discussing the preparative meeting at this point jumbles the hierarchical order, there are reasons for presenting a description here. Many preparative meetings built the meetinghouses, and the locations were shown on the maps of the time. It is very important to know the name of the preparative meeting to which an ancestor belonged for it is then often possible to determine which monthly meeting had jurisdiction, and these monthly meeting records are the important ones for genealogists. The entire pyramid becomes confusing at this level, and an argument could be made for almost any arrangement. Briefly stated, both men's and women's preparative meetings were designed to prepare the business that was to be presented at the monthly meeting. These preparative meetings are rare today. Since the monthly meeting was usually held on Seventh Day (Saturday), the preparative meeting was held in midweek, often following the mid-week meeting for worship. Every effort was made at preparative meetings to separate complaints of a trivial nature from more important matters so that the agenda of the monthly meeting was not overburdened. In addition, the preparative meeting reviewed requests for membership, together with announced intentions of any members who wished to marry. The recommendations for membership came out of the separate men's and women's meetings. The concept of the preparative meeting is important to remember, but it is of academic interest because very few records remain. Preparative meetings held worship sessions each First Day (Sunday) and at mid-week.

Meetings for Worship

This name is misleading since all Friends' meetings were meetings for worship. The term was used when there were enough Friends in the area to conduct worship services but not a sufficient number to justify a preparative meeting. The meeting for worship was held at the appropriate meetinghouse, and was often held in individual homes. Just as with the preparative meetings, the members met for worship on First Day and mid-week. Minutes of these meetings are rare, and a genealogist with limited time should not search for them. Meetings held only for worship were not meant for recording information of any genealogical importance.

Indulged Meetings for Worship

This meeting, indigenous to America, outgrew its usefulness about 100 years ago and therefore no longer exists. It served a real purpose on the frontiers of early America and even later, when the population was being pushed westward. Some groups of Friends, usually just several families, would find themselves close to each other but miles from an organized meeting. Such groups of families were allowed by the nearest monthly meeting to meet at individual homes, although they often grew to the point where construction of a meetinghouse was justified, at which time they became a regular preparative meeting under a monthly meeting. A committee visited the "indulged meeting" regularly to make certain that Quaker principles were adhered to. Because of the temporary nature of these meetings and the remote locations, records of their activities are sparse and, when found, may not contain any information of genealogical use.

Monthly Meetings

Up to this point it might appear that a large amount of space has been used to describe meetings which are not especially valuable to the genealogist. This charge contains elements of truth, but there is a purpose to it. Working with Quaker records without some knowledge of the movement's structure is time-consuming and often ends in a feeling of frustration. In addition, terms used in Quaker records are foreign to other denominations, and you must learn the meanings of certain designations. And it is important to develop an understanding of these expressions until the words and phrases become automatic. These terms must become part of your standard vocabulary, for without them you can be easily misled. Quality must come before quantity, a statement which leads to a discussion of the meeting which constitutes the very heart of Quakerism—the monthly meeting. LEARN THE ELEMENTS OF THIS MEETING WELL, FOR IT IS NOT POSSIBLE TO DO ANY VALID AND COMPREHENSIVE RESEARCH WITHOUT MONTHLY MEETING RECORDS. THEREFORE, IT FOLLOWS THAT THE MONTHLY MEETING OF AN ANCESTOR MUST BE KNOWN BEFORE ANY MEANINGFUL RESEARCH CAN BE DONE. WE CANNOT EMPHASIZE THIS POINT ENOUGH.

There are two general types of monthly meeting records: minutes and registers. These names are self-explanatory, but you must remember that when using microfilm of original records, all the rolls from a single meeting must be examined. For instance, if you are studying New Garden Minutes (an early meeting in Pennsylvania) at a repository, make certain you examine all the rolls of records filmed for this meeting for the time period you are researching. Never assume that the births, deaths, and marriages are not available because they are not on a particular roll. This might seem elementary, but it is easy to forget that you need to look at all the films, particularly in libraries where browsing is not permitted and all materials are brought from the stacks by an employee.

Most of the routine business activities of The Religious Society of Friends were transacted in the monthly meeting, and it is at this point in the organization where extensive minutes were recorded, covering every event which happened in the local Quaker membership. As we have mentioned, a monthly meeting was usually made up of several preparative meetings and, where the area in question has political townships, will usually have the same name as the township in which it is located. The organizational talents of the Friends were put to the test at this point and you must be very careful not to be misled, for it was not unusual for a monthly meeting to bear the same name as the quarterly meeting under whose jurisdiction it fell. To add to the confusion, monthly meetings would sometimes change names. This is particularly true when new meetings were being "set up" as the Quaker membership expanded. You must actually encounter this situation to appreciate the difficulties it causes. This problem is likely to arise in your search, and you need to learn how to sort out the different meetings (see map in Appendix F).

As a general rule, the minutes contain the vital statistics of entire families as long as the members remained within the meeting's geographical boundaries. The neatness of these records, and therefore their ease of use, is directly related to the recording clerk. But, particularly with the very early records, do not expect to find them easy to use. Even with the wealth of information, it would be unusual to trace an individual in a few hours' time. Just as with most old records, the style of handwriting is unfamiliar, the ink is often faded, and indexes are rare. This statement, of course, is true only of the original (primary) records or microfilms of these records and not of the extensive body of secondary works (these are discussed later in Chapter VI). Some of the secondary sources have been printed, although not always published for wide distribution. They are compilations of names and dates from the original records, and they constitute a very large collection. Although these works are far better than none at all, they cannot possibly include the information which makes monthly meeting records unique. It is unfair to say a genealogist can be misled by these abstracted records, but we can state without qualification that names and numbers are sterile. You will not have the opportunity to gain a feel for the things for which the Quakers were willing to endure so much abuse. For instance, formation of committees to reprove a straying soul, along with the reasons for such actions and the names of those appointed to the committees, are reported only in the original monthly meeting records. Simply stated, there is no substitute.

Although the Quakers consolidated their position in the area around Philadelphia, they were destined to carry the concept of the "Inner Light" throughout the inhabited parts of America, often moving in large groups. Hence, a knowledge of their migration routes is a necessity for anyone with a serious interest in Quaker genealogy. The next chapter is devoted to these movements.

CHAPTER IV

PATTERNS
OF MIGRATION AND EXPANSION

The popular image of Quakers, particularly those who lived in colonial America, is that of an ultra-conservative group of people. The picture of a pious family farming the same land for generations is partially true, but it is no more true of the Quakers than of other religious or ethnic communities. The Quakers cannot be accused of being immobile. They were motivated to move onward for a variety of reasons. Some of these reasons were important, though they often seem trivial to us today. The desire for better and less expensive land was probably the primary driving force in most cases. The Quakers, in spite of wanting the "simple life," were not immune to this desire. After all, they were good businessmen, and if their business was not agricultural, it was associated with agriculture in some way. Theirs was an agrarian society and everyone lived with that fact. However, the Quakers had a second motive for moving: their religious zeal and their desire to carry George Fox's concept of the "Inner Light" to less fortunate and uninformed people.

These two forces, plus the desire to escape from those areas in which the institution of slavery was entrenched, resulted in the development of well-established migration trails, first southward to Virginia, the Carolinas, and Georgia, then to the developing Northwest Territory of Ohio and Indiana. These migratory paths were very important to the development of the

35

border states. In fact, by 1850 more than half of Indiana's population was made up of Quakers—generally from the Carolinas. It is therefore essential for researchers in Quaker records to familiarize themselves with these routes of expansion. The hardships endured on these journeys defy belief, but, true to their convictions, Quakers left their paths well marked with meetings. The obsession with organization never faltered and is now of incalculable value to the genealogist. Anyone attempting to follow Quaker ancestors from New England, Pennsylvania, and New Jersey to the Midwest should be fully cognizant of these migration patterns. Unless you study these patterns, you can become thoroughly confused in attempting to reconstruct family movements.

The movement of Quakers to Virginia was not a sudden happening. Even though this migration eventually grew to monumental proportions during the middle of the eighteenth century, it had an early beginning and a long induction period. The first Quaker visitor in Virginia, a woman from London named Elizabeth Harris, came to that area about 1656, more than twenty years before Penn established his colony. The history of the early Quakers who visited Virginia is an interesting story, but it is not of direct genealogical importance. Some of these men and women came directly from England to Virginia and Maryland; others came from the northern colonies. As mentioned earlier, George Fox was an early visitor to both Virginia and North Carolina. The primary goal of almost all these early visitors was to spread Quakerism and to escape the ubiquitous persecutions in Great Britain and New England. But the settlers were not to find an idyllic situation in Virginia, where shipmasters were prosecuted for allowing Quakers to land, and where laws were passed requiring the captains to reboard any Quakers and sail on—the destination not defined. But they kept coming, first one or two at a time, then larger groups, and they all met the same fate: persecution and brutality. Laws were passed forbidding Quakers to meet and discuss current topics with each other. Even saying prayers for the dying was not allowed. The miracle was their persistence. The history of early Quakerism in America is a study in human tenacity.

The progression of Quakerism through Virginia and North Carolina is extremely difficult to separate, since the early immigrants did little to distinguish settlement in the two states. It did not occur in a logical manner, north to south. Rather, the region around the present border between the two states was the first to be populated, probably because the rigorous climate and geography (mainly swampland) precluded outside interference. If one man could be considered responsible for the pattern of settlement it would be William Edmundson, certainly the founder of Quakerism in North Carolina. He first visited America with George Fox in 1672. In April of that year he sailed from Maryland to Virginia and traveled as far south on Albemarle Sound as what is now the city of Hertford in Perquimans County. Here he held the first Quaker services in the wilderness of this unexplored region. Edmundson then returned to southern Virginia, to what is now Nansemond County. The Quaker movement finally took root in this county in the southernmost part of Virginia, and these Virginia Friends provided a destination for the immigrants from New Jersey and Pennsylvania. This is an oversimplification of what became a very complex movement of a particular segment of the entire population. It exposes a genealogist to the special problems in the initial migrations and the destinations of these first southward-bound Quakers.

Since Quakerism demanded organization, it was natural for these southern Friends to search for a meeting to which they could report and from which they could expect support of their efforts to establish themselves on the frontier. As we saw in Chapter III, the entire structure of the Friends movement was built around the concept of meetings of varying function, size, and authority. The Rhode Island Yearly Meeting, the first in America, was established in 1661; later the name was changed to the New England Yearly Meeting. Regular sessions have been held from the beginning, and it is the oldest yearly meeting in the world as regular sessions of the London Yearly Meeting did not begin until 1671. As mentioned previously, the Philadelphia Yearly Meeting was established in 1683 and stretched northward to the New England Yearly and southward to the Carolinas. However, it was 1686 before delegates were sent out to Virginia and the Carolinas from the Philadelphia Yearly; by 1692 a firm relationship had been established. The Society of Friends in South Carolina dates from 1682, when George Fox suggested a union between these Friends and those of North Carolina. At that time the South Carolina Quakers were under the London Yearly Meeting, but the jurisdiction soon changed to the Philadelphia Yearly.

The Quaker population grew gradually in this remote region, and by 1700 a quarterly and three monthly meetings had been established. By this time a Virginia Yearly Meeting had been authorized, followed by the North Carolina Yearly, the records of which begin in 1708. The stage was set for the mass migrations which were to follow.

The large movement southward originated mainly in New Jersey and Pennsylvania. The principal path went through the Monocacy region of Maryland about 1725, crossed the Potomac, and reached Hopewell, Frederick County, Virginia, in 1732. The numbers were sufficient to justify the establishment of the Hopewell Monthly Meeting in 1735. This is an extremely important meeting for researchers in Quaker records since it represented the first stopping place of many members. Fortunately, most of these records have been preserved and published.[6] Another wave of migrating Friends passed from Maryland into Loudoun and Fairfax counties. The Fairfax Monthly Meeting was established in 1745 near the present town of Leesburg.

These migrations were not swift, and families often attended these meetings for several years before moving on. From these areas Quaker settlers continued south through Fauquier, Culpeper, Stafford, and Orange counties, stopping in Campbell,

Bedford, Pittsylvania, and Halifax counties, all in Virginia. The movement then continued south into Surry, Stokes, Guilford, Alamance, Chatham, and Randolph counties in North Carolina, and from there into South Carolina and Georgia. Weeks points out that it is possible to divide this migration into two reasonably well-defined areas: (1) the counties lying on and near the coast, which represented the old Quaker stock; (2) the inland counties, which represented the influx of the later immigrants, many of them Welsh or German.

Although we are skipping a great deal of history, some detail is necessary to keep the story coherent, particularly since so much emphasis will be placed on the need to locate the specific meetings of one's forebears. Friends flourished early in southeastern Virginia, and by 1691 there were Quakers in Norfolk, Nansemond, Southampton, Isle of Wight, Prince George, Charles City, York, Warwick, and Henrico counties. However, this movement expanded slowly and it was 1721 before there was another meeting established, the Cedar Creek Monthly Meeting in Hanover County. This area was the first to decline as a Quaker center. Its Quaker residents became a part of the larger migration, so that by 1736 almost all vestiges of Quakerism had disappeared from the eastern shore of Virginia. Many went into the western counties; still more went south into the Carolinas, first into Perquimans and Pasquotank counties. By 1750 they had crossed Albemarle Sound and settled in what are now Hyde, Beaufort, Craven, Carteret, Jones, Bladen, and Lenoir counties in North Carolina. The Core Sound Monthly Meeting, located in Carteret County, was set up in 1733, and the records of this meeting have been preserved. By this time the movement had turned westward from the eastern tidelands into the more desirable Piedmont region of North Carolina. Newcomers from the North were diverted in this direction, so that the growth of the Piedmont area was extremely rapid compared with that of the coastal regions. Their goal was now Alamance, Chatham, Guilford, and Randolph counties. This part of the migration started around 1740 and continued until about

1775. During this period a large number of Quakers settled on the border between Grayson and Carroll counties, Virginia, near the present town of Galax. Most of these moved to Ohio and Indiana fifty years later, leaving behind very few records.

It is not possible to list all the monthly meetings set up during this time. We refer you to Weeks' book, which not only provides the names of the meetings but often the surnames of the families attending specific meetings. Modern Quaker historians will point out that much research has been done since 1896, when Weeks published his book. This is indeed true, but it does not diminish the value of the book. A researcher looking for Quaker ancestors in southern states should refer to it as a means of ascertaining more exact locations for families.

By 1776 the migration had slowed to the point where only a few isolated families were going into North and South Carolina. In general, this area furnished the Quakers with what they wanted: freedom to worship in their own manner, a minimum of problems with the Indians, and reasonably good land at low prices. They were forced, however, to cope with the institution of slavery, which represented everything obnoxious to them. Historically, from the earliest years in the colonies, Friends had owned slaves and even engaged in the slave trade. Opposition to these practices developed slowly; the anti-slavery movement actually began in the northern colonies in the late 1600s and gained momentum through the first half of the 1700s. However, it was not until 1747 that the movement became a reality in the conscience and testimony of American Friends after visits by John Woolman, the New Jersey Quaker who traveled widely in his ministry against slaveholding and slave trading. Some Southern Quakers became slaveholders through inheritance of large plantations. In Virginia and the Carolinas slavery was an economic and social necessity for the owners after invention of the cotton gin. If these southern Friends did not continue, and the new arrivals did not adopt the practice, they could not compete in a society where manual labor was frowned upon and local legislation made it difficult to free slaves. On the other hand, many Friends could not, nor would they, accept the practice of slavery for their own economic benefit. Thus southern Quakers were confronted with a terrible dilemma and had to make a difficult decision: leave the land they had acquired about fifty years earlier or adopt the "peculiar institution." Some Friends chose to keep plantations and slaves and found a religious home elsewhere. Others, though choosing to remain in the South, manumitted all of their slaves during the landowners' lifetimes, or later, in a will. Many, however, left the South and settled in the new Northwest Territory where slavery was prohibited.

The settlement of the southern states was a slow process, but the movement out of the area took a relatively short time. It started about 1795 and by 1820 was virtually completed. In a sense, it was timely, for the Ordinance of 1785 established a system for disposing of land in the newly acquired Northwest Territory. Acreage was quickly made available at low prices, particularly in Ohio and Indiana. The irony was extended by this development, however, since the Quakers originally had desired to move westward but were blocked by the French and Indian Wars. It is hardly fair to think of their movement south to have been only a temporary diversion, but this is the way it turned out.

What is important to genealogists are the routes chosen for Quaker migrations. Even today we find concrete evidence of their having been in certain locations at one time simply by observing current place names. Naturally, the precise routes depended to a large extent upon the starting places as well as the final destinations. No matter which route was chosen, it was a long and arduous journey. Because of thieves and Indians, a family rarely made the trip alone. They traveled in groups, often sizable, for safety and companionship. It was not unusual for entire groups to be from one meeting. Some of the members dropped out of the large groups and established meetings along the way. In general, four routes were used, and the descriptions of these have been taken directly from Weeks.

- One route was by what was known as the Kanawha road. This led through rough mountainous country for most of the way. Crossing the Dan River, it led by Patrick C[ourt] H[ouse], Virginia, to Marberry's Gap in the Blue Ridge Mountains, thence across Clinch Mountain, by the way of Packs Ferry on the New River, thence over White Oak Mountain to the falls of the Kanawha and down that river to the Ohio, crossing at Gallipolis.

- Another route was known as the Kentucky Road. By this road the traveler crossed the Blue Ridge at Ward's Gap, crossed the New River near Wythe C[ourt] H[ouse], Virginia, thence by way of Abingdon, thence through Cumberland Gap and through Kentucky to Cincinnati.

- A third route was by way of Poplar Camp and Flour Gap; through Brownville and Lexington, Kentucky, and across the Ohio at Cincinnati, Lawrenceburg or Madison. This route was very rough.

- The fourth was known as the Magadee route and lay over the Virginia Turnpike, which had been built from Richmond to the Ohio at the mouth of the Kanawha. This was the favorite route from 1810 until the age of railroads. Emigrants from the eastern part of North Carolina would sometimes go to Richmond direct, while others would strike the pike at Lynchburg or Fincastle, while still others from Carolina

would turn off the pike at Lewisburg,
go by another pike route to Wheeling
and cross the Ohio there. It is said that
as many went by this route as by all
the other routes.[7]

In general, the Quakers from the deep South took the
Kanawha or the Kentucky routes. Virginia Quakers generally
followed what was the Cumberland Road (now U.S. 40) from
Cumberland, Maryland, through the southwestern corner of
Pennsylvania to Washington in that state, on to Wheeling, Virginia (now West Virginia), and from there across the Ohio
River. In navigable months they may have used the Ohio as a
further means of transportation. Several early meetings were
established by these Virginians in Ohio, along the eastern
border not far from the Ohio River. The Carolina Quakers
often went to Tennessee and then through Kentucky to Ohio
and Indiana. This ultimately resulted in Ohio being populated
by Virginia Quakers, and Indiana by those from Carolina via
Tennessee.

For the Virginians, once again the Hopewell Meeting was a
focus. They pressed on to establish meetings in Pennsylvania
at Redstone in Fayette County and at Westland in Washington
County. Both of these meetings were under the direction of the
Hopewell Monthly Meeting, where "certificates of removal"
were issued (see Chapter V for an explanation of this kind of
record). Friends moving on to Ohio before 1800 left their
certificates at either Redstone or Westland. Finally, in 1802,
the Concord Monthly Meeting, located in the present county of
Belmont, was set up in Ohio (not to become a state until 1803).
In all cases, the relevant yearly meeting was Baltimore.

The final settlement of Quakers in Ohio and Indiana is a
complex subject, since at one time the same yearly meeting
controlled Indiana as well as part of Ohio. And at one time
there were three yearly meetings in Ohio, all called, logically
enough, the Ohio Yearly Meeting. (Today there are four, but

only one is called the Ohio Yearly Meeting.) It is a complexity which present-day genealogists find burdensome, and it can be quite discouraging. It is sufficient here to note that there is a pamphlet about early Quakers in Ohio which offers an analysis of the entire situation and puts most of the vagaries into proper perspective.[8] With this pamphlet and Weeks' book referred to earlier, together with numerous articles that have been published on the subject, you will be able to follow the migrations important to Quaker genealogy. We now move into a more interesting area of the Quaker movement—the monthly meeting records and what you may expect to find in these very special records.

CHAPTER V

CONTENTS
OF MONTHLY MEETING RECORDS

Almost by definition, one of a genealogist's principal interests falls under the general category of vital statistics. These constitute the backbone of monthly meeting records and often represent the genealogist's idea of paradise. Yet birth and death records are only the tip of the iceberg. Within the minutes of the monthly meeting these records are sometimes listed by family; in some instances they are in chronological order. You will find that there are usually, but not always, men's meetings and women's meetings. As you might infer from these titles, the meetings were entirely separate. However, this separation was made only for business meetings. Meetings for worship were held in one body. In fact, most meetinghouses were built with a movable partition which could be raised or lowered, as called for by the particular situation. These minutes are interesting if you have time to browse through them, for you often find an ancestor's name mentioned —perhaps appointed to a committee, requesting a certificate of removal to another meeting, or having to answer for some transgression.

Marriage records are particularly important, as it was the Quaker custom for the bride and bridegroom to announce their intentions of marriage to their respective men's and women's meetings. The announcement was made for two consecutive months. A "clearance to marry" was obtained from the meeting

after a report from the committee which investigated the couple
to determine if they were "clear" for marriage, or in other words,
if either the bride or bridegroom had been promised to anyone
else. The report is usually in the minutes and makes interesting,
if not particularly informative, reading. Anyone doing Quaker
research becomes accustomed to committee reports; they are
ubiquitous. It appears the entire Quaker movement was based
upon committee actions, for no part of Quaker life escaped the
close scrutiny of a committee. If the couple were not members
of the same meeting, the marriage took place at the bride's
meeting. In this case, a "certificate of removal" will usually be
found in the minutes of the bridegroom's meeting granting per-
mission to "remove" to the other meeting. In the minutes of the
bride-to-be's meeting will be found the acceptance of this certificate. Then, after one reads of the "intent to marry," and
sometimes the certificate of removal for the man, a certificate
can usually be found for the actual marriage. Later, a report
will be found in the minutes stating that the committee
appointed to attend the marriage has confirmed that the marriage actually took place, giving the date and, at times, the
location where the marriage took place. The "marriage certificate" gives the names of the participants, i.e. the bride and
bridegroom and those present at the time of the marriage. Those
who are new to Quaker research can be confused by a marriage
certificate because the bride signs not with her maiden name,
but with her new married name, for this certificate is written
after the marriage. Relationships are not given in these documents, with the exception that sometimes in the first two or
three lines a parent *may be* named. If several children of the
same family are married over a period of years in the same meeting, it is possible to establish an approximate death date of a
parent. If the parents are named in the first child's marriage certificate and later do not appear for a younger child, or actually
are listed as deceased, you may begin to look for some mention
of the death and burial. The list of witnesses is valuable because
it may include brothers, sisters, parents, aunts, uncles, etc.—in

other words, all those present at the marriage, some of whom may be members of the same meeting, and some of whom may be from the bridegroom's meeting. These names are useful in your research, as they will help establish collateral lines. They may even lead you to a family line which was unknown to you before the certificate was located.

In the monthly meeting records you will encounter two terms, "marriage contrary to discipline" and "marriage out of unity." While these appear to be synonymous, they are distinctly different. "Marriage contrary to discipline" means the couple was married by a civil servant, or by a "hireling priest" (a minister of another religious discipline), while "marriage out of unity" means one of the parties in the marriage was not a Quaker. Either of these conditions was reason enough for the couple to be "disowned" by the Quakers. "Disowned" is a term you will encounter often in meeting records. It means just what you would think—the Society does not want those "disowned" persons attending the meetings. Members could be disowned for many reasons, all detailed in these records. Also noted are names of those appointed to a committee to meet with disgraced members—not once but as many times as necessary—in an effort to convince them of the error of their ways. Once they are repentant, they are invited back to the meeting to admit publicly their wrongdoing. They are then welcomed into the group as full-fledged members once again. Again, all of this activity is fully reported in the monthly meeting minutes, in details not always complimentary to the guilty party.

The fact is, in no other religious organization was it so easy to lose one's membership. Even though the Quakers had no official creed, the organization expected members to live by a discipline dictated by the yearly meeting. Any infraction was reported to the preparative meeting which, in turn, presented it to the monthly meeting. A committee was appointed to investigate the charge and the visits to the offender began. At such time as the culprit was ready to admit wrongdoing, he or she had also to explain the reasons for such heinous actions. Those on the committee would then ask Divine forgiveness and all was forgotten—except for the record in the minutes. However, if the person refused to admit guilt and ask this forgiveness, the committee recommended "disownment." It seems probable that many times these procedures were the only reasons for loss of members from the Society. For instance, in our own research an ancestor disappeared from the minutes about 1812. We finally found a record of a committee being appointed to investigate "fornication" on the part of this man. The name of the woman was given in the minutes. The committee reported several times to the entire meeting that he had been requested to ask forgiveness and admit his guilt. He had temporized, asking for time to think over the entire matter. Finally, after four or five meetings with the committee, this ancestor told them he would prefer to appeal to the yearly meeting for adjudication. In the meantime, while the committee was endeavoring to convince this man of the error of his ways, the woman was petitioning the separate women's meeting to become a full-fledged member of the Society. Such peeks into the lives of ancestors lifts our spirits during long days of unrewarding research. As we mentioned before, personal accounts of Quakers are almost nonexistent, but the vignettes found in these monthly meeting minutes are diamonds to be set in genealogical records. (In the Glossary, you will find a list of terms used in the records.)

By modern standards, some reasons for disownment are trivial. They include:

- deviating from the truth (Quaker tenets)
- keeping liquor in the home
- fighting
- asking high interest on loans
- being seen on the street while a meeting was in progress (we have always wondered *who* was doing the reporting!)

It is this kind of information which makes monthly meeting records particularly valuable, even intriguing. The detail is often more than can ever be expected, and certainly more than can be reasonably transmitted, by a secondary source. The primary records *must* be examined.

Of course, this is not meant to imply that all such records are readily available—or available at all. It is *almost* axiomatic that to maximize the results of your research you must be willing to travel to the repository for the relevant minutes. It is not an absolute necessity, but you are more likely to receive the assistance you need at an official Quaker repository (see Chapters VIII and X). This, of course, is after you have determined the proper site. Only by studying the actual records will you have a full appreciation of the wealth of information the early Quakers left behind. The search is not without its disappointments. Even though the Quakers made a written record of all meeting-related events, such records were not indestructible. Quaker meetinghouses and homes have burned just like many others. Quaker paper and ink of 300 years ago was of no better quality than that of other organizations. Also, unfortunately, all of these records are not in repositories for the convenience of the public. Many Quaker meetings have been very proprietary with their records and, frankly, there are some who will tell you that the records are private and you are not welcome to see them. Fortunately for researchers, even though this situation is frustrating, these meetings are very localized and their lack of cooperation will not really hamper your work. Diligent searching will usually uncover, somewhere, a photocopy made years ago and on deposit in a library. Our experience has been very good, and the person in charge of records at any given locale has assisted us far beyond what might be expected, bringing out records for our perusal, even if the process might take all day. On the other hand, we have been refused—once. Researchers must respond courteously and with due respect for the age and the condition of the records, remembering that in many cases there is only the one copy extant.

We would like to emphasize very strongly that the archivists and librarians at Quaker repositories are your best friends. Use them wisely. They can save you hours and even days. If you are a novice, say so at once. This is neither the time nor place for false pride. Within minutes they will have a good idea of your capabilities anyway. We have always found them extremely informative, with a complete knowledge of Quaker holdings and a willingness, almost a compulsion, to help. There is no point in searching for hours for monthly meeting records in a library which does not even have them. Also, remember that searching a card file in most Quaker repositories is almost an art form. A detailed explanation of this should be first on your priority list of requests. Remember, too, that any questions the person in charge may ask you are meant to elicit the necessary information to aid in your search—not to make you look foolish or to show how little data you have already acquired.

The documentation of the disownment of an ancestor is very important if you spend countless hours perusing records to find a person whose family you are certain was Quaker. It can also be a minor tragedy since, if disownment was accepted by the accused, it means the end of this valuable source of information. Because of the absolute necessity of knowing the subtleties of the Quaker discipline and its ultimate effect on your research, the concept of "birthright Quakers" must be explained. It is really that which is implied by the word: children born to practicing Quaker parents are known as birthright Quakers. However, two married adults with children could join The Religious Society of Friends. This automatically made all minor children Quakers but not birthright members. If the father were disowned, the mother and children remained in good standing in the Society. If you begin finding the names of one parent and the children, without mention of the other parent, you can begin to suspect a death or disownment, and then begin a search in earlier records for documentation of the event.

There is one other type of record which, because of its genealogical importance, deserves special attention. This is the "certificate of removal." If you keep in mind that, above everything else, it is necessary to obtain the name of the monthly meeting your ancestor attended, it is easy to be concerned about what happens when this person moved to a new location. Does this mean the long search for a monthly meeting must start again? The answer is no, but with certain reservations. The certificate of removal takes care of the problem *most* of the time.

The Quakers expanded rapidly in colonial times. The excitement of finding the correct monthly meeting for 1750 might be dashed when you find the family moved to another geographical location or that another monthly meeting had been "set off" from the original meeting. It is almost as though the Quakers had anticipated this potential problem for future genealogists. When a family wished to change locations, a certificate of removal was requested from its present meeting. A committee was appointed to determine if the family affairs were in order. If there were no debts outstanding and if all members of the family were in complete harmony with friends and neighbors, the committee reported that a certificate could be issued. This document could name the father, mother, all the children, the monthly meeting to which they were going, and the date. In some instances, the certificate will read only "John Smith, wife and four children." Of course, the meeting issuing the certificate is named also. The certificate date usually is close to the actual movement of the family, but there are instances where a family moved and then wrote back requesting a certificate for a particular meeting. Several years might have elapsed before all these transactions were accomplished, particularly when a family did not formally request the certificate but their original monthly meeting simply forwarded one to the meeting nearest the place to which they thought the family had relocated. Therefore, the dates on certificates of removal should not be considered absolutely correct. It is often difficult to find certificates of removal if the families moved long distances—particularly to another state—or moved several times. In such cases, the certificate of removal might have remained at the first stopping place, even though most of a person's life may have been spent at another location. However, it is often possible to track an ancestor from meeting to meeting by these certificates of removal. The other side of this coin is that you may never find any certificate from overseas for your immigrant ancestor, and will need to use other means to discover that person's place of origin.

The system had a built-in double check. Not only was a record made of the removal certificate in the minutes of the meeting issuing the certificate but it was also recorded at the other end. This veritable treasure of information was not limited to America. Quakers coming from Wales, Ireland, England, Barbados, or any other place in the world were theoretically required to bring a certificate of removal and, indeed, they did in most cases. Many of these certificates are available for reading, and they are usually the only means of determining where the immigrant originated. They are invaluable for ancestor tracing. On the other hand, as pointed out in the preceding paragraph, they can be misleading. If, for example, a Pennsylvania family moved to Ohio, their certificate was recorded with the monthly meeting nearest their place of residence only after 1802. The first meeting in Ohio was established in December, 1801, at Concord in Belmont County.

With southern Quakers pouring into Ohio beginning about 1800, it was often the case that meetings were not organized in the new territory and certificates would be left at the Redstone or Westland Meetings in western Pennsylvania, through which many of these Quakers traveled. Sometimes the families wrote for their certificates when they were finally settled in their new homes; many times they did not. After meetings were "set off" in the new region, the certificates could not always be sent to the proper meetings.

There is one more warning about using certificates of removal. It was not unusual for a Quaker family to request their meeting in eastern Pennsylvania to send their certificate to a certain location in Ohio. Then, along the way they might have changed their minds about their destination and chosen to settle in another section of Ohio—perhaps 150 miles from where the certificate was sent. Removal certificates, therefore, are not the final answer in tracing Quaker ancestors, but they are extremely valuable tools. We have used them successfully in tracing families coming from Wales and England to the Philadelphia area in 1685, and then moving to Berks County, to western Pennsylvania, to Indiana, and back to Ohio. Used with discretion, they can reduce your searching time by an incalculable amount. All of this discussion about certificates of removal for families applies equally to single persons.

A reminder should be made at this time of a statement in the Preface: this book is only for those searching for ancestors *prior* to 1850. A new set of rules applies after that, but, of course, other record sources exist for the last 100 years which were not available for earlier periods.

Naturally, no record can be examined if it cannot be found. In the case of the Friends, finding records is not always easy. The first step toward helping you in your search is taken in the chapter which follows.

CHAPTER VI

LOCATING AND SEARCHING
MONTHLY MEETING RECORDS

U p to this point we have stressed the fact that you need
to know the monthly meeting to which a Quaker
ancestor belonged in order to find the name you seek. By now,
you are probably asking yourself, "How do I find the meeting
I need when I have no information which even comes close to
giving me a clue?" We hope the steps outlined in this chapter
will provide the answers to your question.

In any genealogical research it is best to work from the
known to the unknown. In Quaker research, perhaps to a
greater degree than in any other type of searching, it does not
pay to skip around in the records. A step-by-step progression
through the records of pertinent monthly meetings will pay
dividends. Therefore, the procedures given below are num-
bered, and you should follow the sequence. This is a method for
locating ancestors who lived before the federal census began in
1790—the most difficult time period for any genealogical
research. This is especially true for Quaker research, as it is so
important to locate a person in a very small area in order to
find the correct monthly meeting. After 1790 the search is
easier since the census will provide county and township information, and sometimes even a town. However, we strongly
advise that these steps be followed regardless of the time period.
This will perhaps eliminate the need to search through county
histories and tax records, and enable you to proceed directly to

maps which show names and locations of monthly meetings within a specific county.

I. *Checking Published Sources*

A. William Wade Hinshaw's *Encyclopedia of American Quaker Genealogy,* six volumes. Each of these volumes contains meeting records for different states: Volume I has North Carolina, South Carolina, Georgia, and Tennessee meetings; Volume II, Pennsylvania and New Jersey; Volume III, New York City and Long Island; Volumes IV and V, southwestern Pennsylvania, Ohio, and one meeting in Michigan; Volume VI, Virginia. Records of Indiana meetings were transcribed by Willard Heiss, a Quaker genealogist, and are sometimes considered a part of this set, although Hinshaw was not living at the time of their publication. These Indiana records comprise Volume VII and are in seven parts, divided as follows: Part 1: Whitewater and Chester Monthly Meetings in Wayne County and Silver Creek-Salem Monthly Meetings in Union County; Part 2: twelve monthly meetings in Wayne, Randolph, and Jay counties; Part 3: fifteen monthly meetings in Grant, Howard, Huntington, Miami, and Wabash counties; Part 4: eleven monthly meetings in Wayne, Henry, and Rush counties; Part 5: fifteen monthly meetings in Orange, Washington, Sullivan, Parke, Morgan, Montgomery, Boone, Tippecanoe, and Vermillion counties, and Vermillion County, Illinois; Part 6: eighteen monthly meetings in Hendricks, Morgan, Marion, and Hamilton counties. (Part 7 is an index.)

The entries are abstracts of meeting records, but they *do not* cover *all* Quaker meetings. We are certainly not downgrading the value of Hinshaw's work, for it is an awesome compilation of names, but the statement is made for the benefit of many researchers who think they might have Quaker ancestors. When surnames cannot be found in Hinshaw, it is natural to discard these volumes as having no value or to stop searching entirely, thinking the original hypothesis is wrong. Either assumption is a mistake.

The volumes are indexed, but these indexes are tedious to use since only surnames are listed. When there are eight or ten lines of page numbers for one surname, discouragement sets in. You can bypass the indexes by turning to the table of contents for each volume. Volumes are divided into sections, with each section covering a specific monthly meeting. By using the table of contents, you can turn directly to a specific meeting section. You will find entries listed chronologically, then alphabetically. Birth and death records are separate from other records, which include marriages, removals, disownments, etc. Be sure you check each type of record for each meeting you search. You will also find separate listings for Orthodox and Hicksite records (for years after 1827, when the schisms occurred). These listings are easy to overlook; however, the table of contents in each volume indicates, under each monthly meeting, the different affiliations (see examples in Appendix B).

If you do find the name for which you are searching, take careful notes of the information contained in the entry. Make certain your notes are detailed and include the abbreviations beside each entry (explanations of these abbreviations are in the front of each book; see our Appendix E as well). The abbreviations will tell you what kind of data you have. Also take careful note of the name of the monthly meeting of which your ancestor was a member. Note also the location, if possible, remembering there is a constant repetition of monthly meeting names from one geographical area to another.

We strongly advise that you read the preface in each volume of Hinshaw's compiled records. Much useful information about The Religious Society of Friends is contained therein. You will find a short history of each meeting at the beginning of the individual sections.

B. There are a number of well-known Quaker genealogies. Consult as many of these as you can.

As emphasized above, *do not* give up your search if you cannot find a name in any of the Hinshaw volumes. Hinshaw's work covers the major meetings in the states he chose to cover; there are many, many meetings, no less important, which are not included in his published volumes. Genealogies, particularly those by Quakers, are a valuable resource. Families often inter-married since they were not allowed to marry outside the Society and remain members unless they made public admission of their wrongdoing.

For Pennsylvania ancestors, consult the works of Gilbert Cope, a Quaker genealogist who prepared a number of gene-alogies; these works were published and may be found in many large research libraries (see Bibliography). As Pennsylvania was the location of a large number of Welsh and English Quakers, the state is a good beginning point for your search. From Pennsylvania most went south and west; some went into Canada.

C. If you have not yet found the name or names for which you are searching, your next step should be to search county histories for the area in which you think your ancestor lived, and try to locate him or her in a specific town or village. This will be of great value in determining the name of the monthly meeting, as most meetings were named for the political town-ship in which they were located. You should make every effort to narrow the locality as much as possible. Often, meetings were within only a few miles of each other. Sometimes, how-ever, the town or village name will not be available. Don't worry about it. The necessary information can be located by other means.

D. Tax records can also be used to determine a specific geographical location for your ancestor. Using the county, township, or a town named in these records, consult gazetteers or other maps which are available in Quaker libraries and which show meetings within a given area (see examples in Appendix F). You will find the names of different meetings on the maps, and, armed with this information, you are ready to check actual meeting records.

II. *Searching Quaker Monthly Meeting Records*

You have now located the name of a monthly meeting to which your ancestor may have belonged, and you are ready to search the microfilm, minutes, or register book of that meeting. There are several methods which may be used in this task. Remember you are not likely to find an index; in fact, if you find one, it will be a rarity.

A. First, look for pages on which you will find a family group listed: the names of both parents, perhaps their birth and marriage dates, and a list of their children with the birth date of each. Early deaths for children will also be recorded. You will, of course, be taking general note of the information on the other pages as you go through the record. If you come across a certificate of marriage for the couple in question, you are now on the right track. Suppose, however, you do not find any other records for this man and woman.

B. The second step in this process should be to look more carefully at the pages preceding the one on which you found the family surname or the marriage record. Read these pages carefully; they will provide valuable information for the next step. Let us suppose the only data you now find is a certificate of removal for the male ancestor stating that his certificate has been accepted from another meeting for the purpose of this marriage. Marriages generally took place in the bride-to-be's meeting, and the bridegroom became a temporary member for the purpose of the marriage. You could continue to search this meeting record for additional information, but it is likely the couple returned to the man's home meeting and a certificate of removal should be located, if possible, for this return. It is possible, of course, that the couple remained in the bride's meeting. If there is no certificate of removal for the couple to the bridegroom's home meeting, continue searching for additional data in the records of the meeting where the marriage took place.

C. If you find a certificate of removal, this step *must* now be followed. Go to the records for the meeting named in this certificate of removal and examine them next. Your goals in searching the new records are (a) to find a record of the removal certificate being given to the man so he could be married in the other meeting; (b) to look for the second certificate of removal from the meeting in which the marriage took place that will return your ancestor and his bride to the bridegroom's meeting. If this is the case (and it probably is if you did not find the family listed in the first set of meeting records), you will then need to search the records of this newly-named meeting for further information which will possibly give you names of children, their marriages, and perhaps death or burial records. Later, you may even find a record of the family's moving to a new meeting.

It is possible to trace a family through monthly meeting records in the step-by-step procedure outlined above, picking up references to the family and its movements. As you do this, look for entries which may name parents and siblings of the pair you are tracking.

We must emphasize that this searching is neither quick nor easy. It takes time and what is infinitely more important, it requires careful reading of sometimes difficult-to-read handwriting. By and large however, we have found the handwriting quite legible. The records were written by the clerk of the meeting and usually the same handwriting appears for a period of time. Therefore, the longer you work the easier it becomes to read the documents.

D. Suppose in the above example you found only a certificate of marriage for your ancestor, and nothing more, after having read through the meeting records very carefully. Before abandoning your search, ask the librarian where you are working if there happened to be a new preparative meeting set up under the jurisdiction of the meeting in which you found the marriage recorded. Your family might be attending this new preparative meeting, yet no certificates would be issued because in reality a "removal" did not actually take place. Instead, look for minutes of the first meeting for this new group in which you may find a membership roster. If there is such a new meeting, then proceed through those records as outlined in steps A-C.

E. Depending upon the results you have from the steps outlined above, you may continue through the records from meeting to meeting (there was a great amount of movement among meetings). If these steps do not produce even a single mention of the particular ancestor for whom you are searching, you may conclude that perhaps one parent of this person married a non-Quaker. If this is the case, the local courthouse of the county in which the meeting was located should be the focus of your next step, as there may be a civil record of the marriage. When a Quaker and a non-Quaker were married, a justice of the peace or a minister of a denominational church could have performed the ceremony. Any Quaker who married a non-Quaker would be automatically disowned (unless he or she could prove good reasons for the marriage). If such were the case, then a record may exist in the appropriate courthouse.

If you find a civil record, then you may look for a record of the matter being taken up in the appropriate business meeting. As in any other genealogical research, dates when marriages were required to be recorded vary with each state, and it is advisable to check the state/county laws.

III. *Additional Searching*

If you believe your ancestor was at one time a Quaker but you still cannot find him, there are some additional steps you may take.

A. We mentioned at the beginning of this chapter the records published by William Wade Hinshaw. However, the Friends Historical Library, Swarthmore College, Swarthmore, Pennsylvania, has a large collection of unpublished Hinshaw records. These were a part of William Wade Hinshaw's collection but they were not ready for publication at the time of his death, and his estate donated the collection to this library. You are free to work in the library, using this group of records as well as other materials in the Quaker collection. If you cannot visit personally, the library will advise you of the best procedure to follow for your particular needs and will be able to recommend local researchers who can assist you. These records have also been microfilmed and are available through the LDS in Salt Lake City (see Chapter XI).

In Hinshaw's unpublished records, it is possible to find names not easily located in his published volumes or in meeting records (you may be looking in the wrong records). These unpublished records include many early meetings and generally cover earlier dates than are found in the published volumes. They also cover meetings which were located in states outside the original thirteen colonies or states, including some west of the Mississippi River, for which the time periods are much later.

B. Once you have located an ancestor in a monthly meeting record you should not assume the most difficult research is behind you.

The Religious Society of Friends was a mobile society. Its members traveled from meeting to meeting, often for the purpose of reporting to a home meeting on the current status of the meetings visited. In other cases, visiting members were considered ministers, and might be visiting other communities to assist them in their spiritual life. We have one ancestral line in which successive generations produced several ministers, men as well as women. These Quaker ministers moved back and forth between meetings with great abandon—or so it seems to us today when we are trying to follow them in the records.

In all of these instances, certificates of removal were issued from the home meeting to the other meetings. Careful searching of the records discloses the appointment of such a member to undertake the journey; the certificate of removal will usually be found very near the appointment date.

Sometimes you will find a certificate of removal that will give the name of the new location but will not give the reason for the change. In these cases, the records may be searched for the business meeting in which the issue was taken up by the entire membership.

IV. *Church Archives*

In the 1930s, before World War II, the Works Projects Administration of the United States Federal Works Agency began a program to inventory the archives of the different religious denominations. There are individual state volumes of these inventories, but, unfortunately, the records of only three states were completely inventoried and published for the Quakers: Rhode Island (1939); New York (1940); and Pennsylvania. The volume for Pennsylvania was published in 1941 and is entitled *Inventory of Church Archives, Society of Friends in Pennsylvania.* It was published in collaboration with the Friends Historical Association and distributed by Friends book stores in Philadelphia. All these WPA volumes are invaluable reference sources for locating meetings in these three states. Not only will you find a history of the individual meetings, but in each case you will find listed the records extant at the time of the publication. Many of the records have been transferred to other locations since publication; however, these three volumes are excellent aids in your research. You will be able to find exact locations of meetings and the years of active operation for each meeting. Look for these volumes in Quaker libraries, state and large city libraries, and historical society libraries; you may even find them in larger university libraries.

V. *A Word of Caution*

You cannot always depend upon finding the information you need. Even though removal certificates were issued, they were sometimes left at meetings other than the ones to which they were addressed, or they were lost, or they were left at the correct meeting but the person or persons named in the certificate went to another meeting without the certificate.

If a certificate of removal cannot be found, the only recourse left is to search civil records within the same general area in an effort to discover a change of residence to a nearby township or county. With this new information, you will be able to locate the closest meeting and proceed as outlined.

The research plan outlined in this chapter will generally produce the best results with a minimum amount of wasted time and effort. Much depends upon the amount of preliminary work which has been done in the published Hinshaw volumes, as well as in published genealogies, etc. In Chapter VII you will learn about some problems you may encounter while using Quaker records. In Chapters VIII and X, Quaker record repositories for the United States, Canada, and Great Britain are listed with a description of the holdings of each. In Chapter IX we list historical societies and libraries which have Quaker material. These are not Quaker institutions, but all of them provide sources for you to check, and some of the holdings of each one are listed. And in Chapter XI we discuss the Quaker resources of the Church of Jesus Christ of Latter-day Saints— how to locate microfilm of a monthly meeting record in the catalogues and indexes of a LDS library and how to order the film.

CHAPTER VII

QUAKER RECORDS
AND SOME POSSIBLE PROBLEMS

The richness of many Quaker records makes the uninitiated researcher wonder if there is any detail that cannot be found. When the appropriate meeting records are being studied, the data flows so rapidly that it is easy to become euphoric as you systematically piece entire families together from these primary records. You may spend hours doing this. However, most of your time will be spent tracing the children who moved to other meetings, through a marriage or for other reasons. Since the records are so complete, you feel encouraged to continue working. We have all experienced the enthusiasm of successful research. However, few dreams result in a perfect ending, and this is certainly true of Quaker records, mainly because Friends steadfastly rejected certain practices common to other denominations. For instance, the basic rituals of baptism, marriage, and burial were not part of the Quaker beliefs. They considered rituals ostentatious and believed such practices should be kept out of Quaker life.

Marriages were accomplished without the assistance of a minister. The couple merely stood before the entire meeting, agreed to become man and wife, and then signed the certificate. Through the two previous declarations of intent before the entire meeting, the reports by the appointed committee members, and the marriage in the bride's monthly meeting, absolutely no doubt could remain that the marriage did indeed take place. The committee reported on the couple's "clearness" for marriage. This simply meant that neither party was already married nor had either promised to marry someone else. By these public acts they were considered to be married in the sight of God and by the community in which they lived. The amount of peripheral information obtained in reading through this chain of required events far exceeds that available from any other religious group, mainly because those present signed as witnesses.

You should keep in mind that since there were no rituals you will never find a baptismal record of a Quaker and you will not find mention of a funeral service. Another waste of time is looking for tombstones of the very early Quakers. They believed such a practice unseemly, pompous, and therefore sinful. The minutes will give the death and burial dates but there will be no eulogy. You will occasionally find "memorials," but these were written only for the most prominent of Quakers, those who stood out from the general membership through exemplary personal lives or because of unusual sacrifices they made for their beliefs. Any personal reference was considered an abomination, so in order to learn what kind of person a certain Quaker ancestor was, you must look beyond the minutes of the meeting, into county histories—or perhaps into civil records, for being a Quaker did not absolve that person from following the laws. Hence, deeds, wills, court actions, taxes, etc. may be located for an ancestor, but these records are all found in the courthouses of the county of residence.

When a name is found on several committees, you may draw some conclusions regarding the prominence of that person in the local meeting and community, as well as the piety of the man or woman. It is often possible to find this same person listed in later minutes as a "minister," even though the Quakers did not officially employ ordained ministers. This term refers more to the willingness of a person to speak wisely in meeting and, perhaps even more, reflects the willingness of the members of the meeting to listen. It is sometimes possible to find the "memorials" mentioned in the last paragraph written about such ministers when they were deemed to be extraordinarily gifted speakers and were considered to be especially endowed with the "Inner Light." Personal information is not included in these memorials, except for occasional special incidents in the members' lives.

Another pitfall for the purist can be the unique way the Quakers dated events. They did not use names for days of the week or months of the year since most of these names were derived from the names of pagan gods. A date such as August 19, 1748 will never be found. Rather it would be written "19th da 6th mo 1748." Sometimes this will be written as 6mo 19da 1748. Why 6th month since August is the 8th month? The Quakers, along with everyone else in the American Colonies and England, did not begin using the Gregorian calendar until 1752. Under the Julian calendar the year began on March 25th; March was the first month and February the twelfth month. This is something of a problem when an event occurred in the months of January, February or up to March 25th, for then the date is given as 1748/1749. Such a dating practice satisfied everyone, including civil authorities, if for instance an inheritance was being established.

You may find that some legal documents will read "the 8th mo 5th da 1748 in the month called October." It is disconcerting when a date such as 30th da 11th mo 1722/1723 is found. The double year indicates that the old calendar was in use. Even though the Gregorian Calendar was adopted in 1582, as mentioned above it was 1752 before the change was universally accepted. We are emphasizing this point here so that if exact days, months, and years are wanted, the old Quaker records must be used with great caution. Remember that until 1752 "1st mo" is March.

We would like to point out also that you may find secondary material (genealogies are a case in point) in which the compiler transcribed dates incorrectly—for instance, "30th da 11th mo 1738/1739" rewritten as "Nov. 30, 1738/39" when the date in question is actually "30th January 1738/1739." The dual year must be used until you are quite certain the locale in question has adopted the Gregorian calendar (or until the Quaker records no longer have the dual form or the year is after 1752). Dual dating is applicable *only* for the first three months (to 25 March) of the present calendar and *not* for the other nine months. The first date given is the Julian year, the second the Gregorian year. Another way of finding whether the old Quaker method of dating is being used in any given set of records is to search back and forth until a month such as the "2nd mo" is found and then see if any entries were made on either the 29th or 30th days. If this was done, then you will know the old system was being used and the month would be the present month of April rather than February. Other months can be used. For instance, if it is the "7th mo" and you find the "31st," you would know the new system is being used and the month is our present month of July rather than the Quaker September.

For the benefit of those who are searching for Welsh ancestors, we would like to emphasize some words of caution. First, the Welsh commonly used double names such as James James or Thomas Thomas. This is disconcerting when you are using indexes, and following a single family can be a major research problem. Even worse is the patronymic method using the word "ap" for "son of." Thus, Hugh ap Thomas means Hugh son of Thomas, except *this* Thomas is a *given* name, not a surname. You may be looking at records where the given names go back several generations, but you will not have any information as to the particular family group involved, e.g. Hugh ap Thomas ap John ap James ap David ap Evan. After a few generations where "ap" is used, it is as though you were looking into a battery of mirrors. There is no equivalent practice in any other country. It is not similar to Ludwig von Beethoven since in this case "Beethoven" is a surname. Fortunately, once in America the Welsh dropped this practice, but often it can be a problem with the immigrant generation. Actually, it may be more complicated than outlined above, as entire names were sometimes changed, e.g. the sons of a John ap Thomas took the surname of Jones (from the given name John) rather than the surname Thomas; however, this practice was relatively rare.

We have pointed out in an earlier chapter that personal information is very difficult to find. Descriptions of height, weight, color of hair and eyes, along with the myriad details we would all like to find about our ancestors, will never be found in Quaker records. Quakers believed man was placed on earth for a greater purpose than self-aggrandizement. While a great deal of space is often given in the records to preliminaries before the actual entry appears, this space is never taken up with personal histories. Perhaps records come closest to personal facts when someone is required to leave the meeting because of violation of a basic tenet. The offense is described, often in considerable detail. You may then speculate about the offender's personality. Also, on rare occasions, certain platitudes about the goodness of the person will be used, but anyone experienced in using Quaker records soon learns not to use these entries to evaluate a specific family member. The same words are used too frequently. As a general rule, any record of a personal nature is usually negative, not positive. Naturally, there are no pictures or drawings.

Some other records you will not find are personal business records, entries of personal donations to the monthly meeting, property holdings, mention of guardianship proceedings, and entries about military service. Pacifism was and is part of the Quaker doctrine. All members were expected to refuse any kind of service which required bearing arms against another person. It is a historical fact that a few Quakers served in the Revolutionary and Civil Wars, but civil and military government records should be used to prove the service. There are no monthly meeting records describing members enlisting in, or returning from, any military service.

One more point about the information you will not find in Quaker records: although certificates of removal are of the utmost value in tracing the movements of families or groups of Quakers, these certificates may never give the exact reason for moving. The wording is always so vague that you can read almost any meaning into it. These entries are very frustrating, particularly when you are researching an ancestor who immigrated to America from Europe. Most researchers want to know the reasons for these moves, particularly in the late 1600s when large numbers of Quakers arrived in America.

During the early part of the 1800s, The Religious Society of Friends experienced internal problems. We will not go into detail for two reasons. First, as stated in the Preface, this book applies to the use of records prior to 1850. Many changes in the Society occurred after that date and it is often better to trace Quakers in civil records after 1850. Second, all the changes do not affect the work of the genealogist. Records were continued in much the same manner. However, you should be aware of certain terms and the ramifications inherent in them.

The main location of the first change was Philadelphia Yearly Meeting, and the first critical years are 1827 and 1828. The basic problem was one of interpretation of George Fox's teachings on the capability of every man to be his own minister. A Quaker from Long Island, New York, named Elias Hicks believed that Friends were diverging from the original concepts of George Fox's teachings of the individual's freedom to believe only in revealed Truth and to follow the Inward Light. The ensuing controversy resulted in a division into two groups, the Hicksites and the Orthodox. The entire Quaker movement suffered from this schism, and what for 150 years had been an exemplary organization was now split into two factions.

In the 1840s and 1850s the Orthodox segment was torn again, this time by John Wilbur, a New England Friend, and Joseph John Gurney of London Yearly Meeting. Naturally enough, their followers were called Wilburites and Gurneyites. And in the late nineteenth century another schism occurred and the Orthodox Gurneyites divided into Progressive and Conservative factions. The name "Orthodox" is confusing to the entire picture since the general inclination is to think of them as disciples of George Fox. (There are histories available which do much to clarify our understanding of the schisms in the Friends' organization, and you will find some of these listed in the Bibliography.) Without a doubt, it would have been better for the Quakers had these substantial changes not occurred. Of lesser importance, the splits make life for the genealogist more confusing. Each group believed it was *the* group. For instance, at one time there were three Ohio Yearly Meetings and five New York Yearly Meetings.[9] It is best to ask any Quaker library which records they have. Usually the Quaker repositories do not limit their holdings and have all the records under the yearly meetings they represent. On the other hand, there are some locations with records from only one branch of the Society.[10]

Another problem is the fact that there are duplications in names of the monthly meetings under any given yearly meeting. For instance, there are records for Abington Monthly Meeting–Hicksite, and Abington Monthly Meeting–Orthodox. Extreme care must be taken when you are using Quaker records, for it is so easy to overlook the designations and to become confused. However, do not become discouraged—you will be able to learn the differences and to find the information you need. From a genealogist's point of view, actual use of the records does not vary because of the local affiliation. We have discussed the separations which occurred in the latter half of the nineteenth century only for your information and not for the purpose of making your research difficult. The records will indicate the group involved.

One of the difficulties in using Quaker records is that some repositories contain vast amounts of Quaker material while others have but few holdings. To group all these repositories together would be misleading. In order for you to set priorities, these libraries and depositories are discussed in separate chapters. The next chapter is devoted to institutions which have major Quaker holdings.

CHAPTER VIII

QUAKER REPOSITORIES FOR RECORDS

Authentic and original Quaker records are found in official Quaker repositories. A number of these repositories are located across the United States. The list which follows is as complete as we have been able to make it. We have tried to include all the major locations, but we take full responsibility for any omissions. However, we feel that you will find a gold mine at each location listed here.

We begin the list in Pennsylvania, as this state probably contained more Quakers at one time than any other state, and also because we look upon Pennsylvania as the "ancestral home" of the majority of Quakers and their descendants in the United States.

The Friends Historical Library, Swarthmore College, Swarthmore, Pennsylvania 19081

The Friends Historical Library was founded in 1871 specifically for the purpose of preserving the records of the many monthly meetings under the jurisdiction of the Philadelphia and Baltimore Yearly Meetings. In addition, meetings in northern Virginia are included in the collection. This is the largest collection in the world of Quaker meeting archives, either in the original manuscripts or on microfilm.

The collection at Swarthmore constitutes a vast resource for the genealogist. The Quaker archives include records of more than 140 quarterly, monthly, and preparative meetings in Pennsylvania, New Jersey, Delaware, and Virginia. These records include minutes of men's and women's meetings for business, minutes of ministers' and elders' meetings, and registers of births, deaths, marriages, and removals. In addition, there are manuscripts, published genealogies, maps, photographs, books, pamphlets, periodicals, family papers, journals of Quaker ministers, and miscellaneous records. The William Wade Hinshaw Index to Unpublished Quaker Records, consisting of 285,000 three-by-five-inch cards, is housed in a large cabinet area. The cross-index is by family surname only. These records cover sixteen states other than those listed above and represent a valuable source for locating family members belonging to seventeen early meetings under the Philadelphia and Baltimore Yearly Meetings, as well as later records for the Midwest and the West. Also included in Swarthmore's holdings are British Quaker records and manuscripts, including minutes of London Yearly Meeting and the Meeting for Sufferings, and epistles. Copies of meeting records (birth, death, and marriage registers) for Great Britain, including Wales and Ireland, are on microfilm. These records may also include certificates of removal. There are records of Ohio and Illinois Yearly Meetings (Hicksite) and microfilm copies of minutes and registers of many meetings in New England, New York, and North Carolina.

The Historical Library at Swarthmore also has significant holdings of writings by and about prominent Friends and about the Quaker movement, along with books on the local history of the Delaware Valley and Maryland, colonial Pennsylvania, Puritanism, the English Revolution, and the Mennonites. The total collection comprises 34,000 books, pamphlets, and serials; 255 manuscript collections; and 4,000 volumes of original meeting records.

For additional information, contact the library. The librarians do not do research but will assist you on a personal visit or will recommend local researchers. There is no charge for using the library.

The Quaker Collection, Haverford College Library, Haverford, Pennsylvania 19041

Haverford's Quaker Collection is primarily one of published works by Quaker authors. The holdings include many old and rare out-of-print works. They do have some actual meeting records for the Philadelphia Monthly Meeting, together with histories of the meetings. This collection is more for historians than genealogists.

The collection contains rare Quaker tracts and the writings of George Fox, William Penn, and other early prominent Quakers; also journals, manuscripts, necrologies, Quaker periodicals and newspapers, as well as printed minutes of yearly meetings, both from America and overseas. It includes indexes of death notices published in four Philadelphia Friends periodicals; an index of Quaker biography; and a reference index which contains biographical, historical, and subject references to articles in various sources. Haverford also has maps, photographs, and pictures of early Pennsylvania, New England, and other areas where Quakers have been active. Finally, you will find legal documents of various description, family papers, and a sizable collection of autograph papers. In addition to all of the foregoing, Haverford houses many other small collections of interest to the scholar. There are 25,000 printed volumes in addition to the manuscript collection, along with 465 reels of microfilm which include records of London Yearly Meeting; the Swarthmore (England) Manuscripts of Friends House Library; records of many United States Friends meetings (particularly New York and New England); anti-slavery publications; and some unpublished doctoral dissertations.

The library does not do research, but you may use the facilities on a personal visit. Write for further information.

Haverford and Swarthmore are only about ten miles apart.

Pendle Hill Library, Pendle Hill,
Wallingford, Pennsylvania 19086

The Quaker collection at Pendle Hill is very limited. They are located only a short distance from Swarthmore and therefore use the records at the Friends Historical Library. Pendle Hill is a publishing house for Friends.

Friends Historical Collection of Guilford College,
Greensboro, North Carolina 27410

Friends Historical Collection at Guilford is the depository for the surviving records of meetings in North Carolina, beginning with the earliest known minutes of Perquimans Meeting in 1680. It holds the original minutes and records of the thirty-three oldest North Carolina meetings which are abstracted in Volume I of William Wade Hinshaw's *Encyclopedia of American Quaker Genealogy*. In addition to nineteen microfilm reels of extant minutes and records of meetings belonging to Virginia Yearly Meeting, Guilford College also houses records of other meetings for the southeastern part of the United States, personal and family papers, printed material by and about Friends worldwide, and materials on Quaker history. It also includes genealogies and manuscript files on family surnames.

Research is done on a limited basis and personal research, for which there is a small fee, may be done by making advance arrangements. Write the library for additional information.

Quaker Collection, Everett L. Cattell Library,
Malone College, 515 25th Street, N.W.,
Canton, Ohio 44709

The Cattell Library's Quaker Collection includes records for meetings under the Ohio Yearly Meeting, along with records for a very few meetings from as early as 1801 and 1804. However, most of the records are from the mid-1800s and later. There are at least three meetings in which the records date from 1814 and 1820.

Records for the mid-1800s and later are for meetings which range from North Carolina to Michigan, and for some meetings in western (later) and in eastern (early) Ohio. This collection also contains minutes and records from the twentieth century.

At the present time these records are being catalogued and shelved for use by visitors. Since they are not readily available to researchers, you should contact the library and inquire about the accessibility of the collection before even contemplating a visit. Librarians do not do research at this time, but they will answer a short mail inquiry.

Quaker Collection, S. Arthur Watson Library, Wilmington College, Wilmington, Ohio 45177

The Quaker Collection at Wilmington covers primarily southwestern and southcentral Ohio, some of Indiana, and parts of Illinois. The coverage represents monthly, quarterly, and yearly meetings under the Wilmington Yearly, the Ohio Valley Yearly, and the Illinois Yearly Meetings. Ohio Valley was formerly the Indiana Yearly Meeting. The earliest records date from 1768 and are from the Miami Monthly Meeting.

The collection contains approximately 7,000 volumes on Quaker history, philosophy, thought, and practice from 1700 to the present; several hundred pamphlets, tracts, epistles, and rare books; Friends periodicals; and minutes from twenty-four yearly meetings across the United States.

In addition, there are about 200 volumes of genealogy and family history, covering parts of Pennsylvania, New York, Massachusetts, the Carolinas, and Virginia, as well as Ohio. They also have Quaker reference books and some unpublished manuscripts relating to Ohio. Most of the meeting records in this collection have been filmed by the LDS Library in Salt Lake City, Utah (see Chapter XI).

Research may be done personally, without charge, or by mail, for which there is a fee. Write the library for information before making a visit in person, as there are times during the year when the facility may be closed.

Quaker Collection, Lilly Library, Earlham College, Richmond, Indiana 47374

The Quaker Collection at Earlham College contains some minutes of monthly meetings. Outside the Philadelphia area, however, it has the largest collection of printed minutes of yearly meetings from all over the world, consisting of approximately 10,000 volumes, all reasonably well indexed. Generally, the beginning dates are in the 1800s. None of these minutes are on microfilm but they are available to the public. In addition to the yearly meeting records, this collection includes biographies, periodicals, writings by and about Friends, sermons and tracts of the nineteenth and twentieth centuries, essays and epistles of the seventeenth and eighteenth centuries, histories of the Quaker movement, including the separations, for America and for some foreign countries, genealogies and obituaries, published and private journals, memoirs, and published works by and about the Society of Friends on a variety of general and specialized subjects, together with published fiction, poetry, and drama by and about Friends.

Haviland Records Room, 222 E. 16th Street, P.O. Address: 15 Rutherford Place, New York, New York 10003

Haviland Records Room is the official archives for the New York Yearly Meeting and has original records only for meetings under that yearly. They have abstracts of one Monroe County, three Westchester County, five Dutchess County, and two Columbia County monthly meetings. These alphabetical abstracts, prepared by Willard Heiss from handwritten notes in a format similar to Hinshaw's volumes, contain abstracted records of marriages and transfers into a meeting, but often do not contain requests for membership or transfers out. They also may not show movement of members between meetings. Abstracts for some meetings in northern New Jersey are also available in the same format.

Included in the holdings at this location are four volumes of compilations of marriage data for New York Yearly Meeting from the earliest extant records to about 1850.

A very few of the records have been indexed, but no central surname index exists for the entire collection. Some of the monthly meeting records under New York Yearly are on microfilm and cover years up to 1850. The Records Room has copies, and the reels are also available through the LDS in Salt Lake City (see Chapter XI).

In addition to these records, Haviland has a set of notebooks with cemetery records for some but not all the burying grounds of the area covered by New York Yearly Meeting, together with printed genealogies of Quaker families.

There is a fee for personal research and an hourly charge if you write requesting assistance. No photocopying will be done. It is advisable to write before visiting, as the Records Room is open on a limited basis.

Archivist, New England Yearly Meeting,
Rhode Island Historical Society Library,
121 Hope Street, Providence, Rhode Island 02906

Records of the New England Yearly Meeting, which includes the Rhode Island Quarterly Meeting, are on approximately 170 rolls of microfilm at this library. The records generally date from the 1700s (one of the meetings is in Nova Scotia), although in one instance certificates of removal begin in 1647 for the Rhode Island Monthly Meeting, and there are a few records for the last quarter of the 1600s. The records also extend into the twentieth century.

Indexes are rare, but they do exist for some of the meetings. The Quaker Archivist is available one day a week, and should be contacted by mail. The library is free and open to the general public, and the Quaker microfilm is available to library visitors. In the summer the library is open weekdays at different hours; during the winter it is closed on Mondays but is open Tuesday through Saturday.

New England Quaker Research Library, Librarian, P.O. Box 655, North Amherst, Massachusetts 01059

This library is located in the Mt. Toby Friends Meeting House, Leverett, Massachusetts, on State Route 63, about four miles north of North Amherst. The holdings consist mainly of books and pamphlets, 2,800 of which have been classified; about 3,000 more await classification. The library is open when the meetinghouse is being used or by appointment with the librarian.

Quaker Collection, Friends University Library, 2100 University Avenue, Wichita, Kansas 67213

The Quaker Collection of Friends University Library in Wichita has extensive holdings of Quaker material. The archives of Kansas Yearly Meeting (now Mid-America Yearly Meeting), 1872 to the present, as well as the archives of the Kansas Yearly Meeting—Conservative, 1879-1929, are a part of the collection. Some of the Kansas Yearly Meeting records date from the 1860s for meetings set up by Indiana Yearly Meeting. The Kansas Yearly Meeting includes meeting records from Alaska, Nebraska, Missouri, Oklahoma, Colorado, and Texas. Not included are meeting records from Arkansas.

The library also has volumes of abstracts taken from the unpublished Hinshaw collection at Swarthmore, as well as Indiana abstracts prepared by Willard Heiss. In addition to these resources, there are books on the Quaker migration to America; biographies; burial and cemetery records for Indiana, Iowa, Kansas, North Carolina, and Ohio; genealogies; histories of specific geographical areas through which Quakers traveled; accounts of the yearly, quarterly, and monthly meetings; cemetery records of the area, along with memorials; and yearly meeting minutes and monthly meeting records for each area covered. There are marriage records in abstract form, in Quaker periodicals and in some published volumes. The memorials of ministers and prominent Friends are in yearly meeting minutes, in archive files, and in published form covering Baltimore, the Philadelphia, New Jersey, and New York areas, New England, Ohio, and Kansas. Some obituaries are available which have been taken from published Quaker periodicals. Along with a group of miscellaneous sources, there are also some published sources from Great Britain.

The Quaker Collection is open when the main library of the University is open and is closed during school breaks. An appointment should be made in advance if you are from out of town, as researchers are assisted by members of a volunteer staff who are not always available.

Quaker Collection, Wilcox Library,
  William Penn College,
  North Market Street, Oskaloosa, Iowa 52577

The Quaker Collection of William Penn College contains several family histories, some of which cover early Quaker immigrants from the Eastern and Southern Seaboard. Included in the library's holdings are the William Wade Hinshaw volumes, Willard Heiss's Indiana books, and some Miami Valley of Ohio records—transcribed and in published form. All of the foregoing should be considered as secondary source material.

Monthly meeting records for the Iowa Yearly Meeting (Friends United Meeting) are located at the Yearly Meeting Office. There is a charge for opening the record vault in addition to an hourly charge for searching by the archivist. The records are not complete, as some local meetings have retained their records. The yearly meeting address is listed in Appendix G.

The library is open weekdays, with short hours on Saturdays and Sundays. Vacation hours are announced periodically.

Quaker Collection, Wardman Library, Whittier College, Whittier, California 90608

The Quaker Collection at Whittier College has limited genealogical value. There are genealogies, regional histories, death notices from Quaker periodicals, Hinshaw's *Encyclopedia*, and several volumes for specific monthly meetings (two of which are in Indiana, three in Maryland, and one in New York), together with four books which cover some meetings in Virginia. A few English records are transcribed in four volumes. The library also has a collection of yearly meeting minutes and a few general books about the early Quakers in America.

The library requests that advance notice be given before a visit, so that a staff member will be available.

Quaker Collection, Shambaugh Library, George Fox College, Newberg, Oregon 97132

Shambaugh Library's Quaker Collection consists of a small number of published Quaker genealogies, together with a group of books of general interest, some of which are histories while others are about Quaker families in different areas of America. As in most Quaker collections, Hinshaw's *Encyclopedia* is available in the library.

The Northwest Yearly Meeting archives are in the vault of the Newberg Friends Church and in the Church Archives Room in Sutton Hall, on the college campus. While almost the entire archives date from the early 1900s, there are some records from the last quarter of the nineteenth century for early meetings in Oregon. Records of monthly meetings (or local churches), Ministry and Oversight (counsel), Sunday School, and Christian Endeavor (youth) records are included.

Local Monthly Meetings

Many of the Friends meetinghouses active today have retained the records of their respective meetings. You may be able to gain access to the records for the meeting you are interested in by contacting the clerk of that meeting. The archives at the following location in Indiana are extensive and represent a large number of meetings:

First Friends Meeting House
East Main and Fifteenth Streets,
Richmond, Indiana 47374

First Friends Meeting House has original records for southwestern Ohio, some parts of Michigan, and Indiana if the meetings were under the Indiana Yearly Meeting. They have a card file, arranged geographically under the name of each meeting, in which minutes with births and deaths are partially indexed. The earliest records date from the early 1800s. Write to the meetinghouse before visiting; it does not have a library. Only one person is in charge of these records and must be contacted before any research is performed. Specific questions will be answered, and there is a charge for postage and for copying.

Yearly Meetings

The yearly meeting of a state or larger area will be able to furnish information on monthly meetings under its jurisdiction. It is possible that smaller, individual collections of records may be located by writing to the yearly meeting for the area in which you are interested. These meetings are listed in Appendix G.

From time to time while working in non-Quaker libraries you may find records which are listed in a card catalogue as "Quaker Records." In all probability the listing is for transcribed records. There are instances of photocopies on deposit for one meeting, which cover only a few years, although occasionally a few original records are to be found in the manuscript collections of state archives. We have stressed throughout this book that *only* monthly meeting records will contain genealogical data of any value to a family researcher. In the next chapter we discuss several locations other than Quaker repositories where you may find Quaker material.

CHAPTER IX

HISTORICAL SOCIETIES AND LIBRARIES WITH QUAKER MATERIAL

The archives and libraries of historical societies, and state or public libraries, may have microfilm or transcripts of Quaker records. In some cases, you may even find some original Quaker records among the manuscript collections of these societies. While these are not official Quaker repositories, they may enable you to begin your research without traveling too far from home. It is impossible in this book to give all of these locations, but we shall list a few to get you started, as some of the larger ones are especially rich in Quaker material. Please include a stamped, self-addressed envelope when writing for information.

Historical Society of Pennsylvania, 1300 Locust Street, Philadelphia, Pennsylvania 19107

The Genealogical Society of Pennsylvania, 1300 Locust Street, Philadelphia, Pennsylvania 19107

The libraries of these two organizations are combined at the one location and constitute an enormous collection, not only for Quaker research but for general research, genealogical as well as historical. Here you will find published genealogies of Quaker families by Gilbert Cope, a prominent Quaker genealogist at the turn of the century who lived at West Chester,

Pennsylvania, and had access to the Quaker records of Chester, Delaware, Bucks, Berks, Lancaster, and Montgomery counties, as well as the city and county records for Philadelphia. The library has large manuscript collections from the genealogical files of Cope and several other Quaker researchers who lived and worked in the same area.

The card catalogues of two societies' combined collections are extensively cross-indexed. They are separated into many categories and divided further by fairly narrow subjects. These card files provide a storehouse of opportunities for the researcher. The societies also have an extensive collection of more than 2,500 published genealogies—not all Quakers, of course. In addition, there is material of general interest to the researcher.

A daily fee is charged to non-members. Write or call for information about research by the staff and the hours the libraries are open.

State Library of Pennsylvania, General Library Bureau, Box 1601, Harrisburg, Pennsylvania 17126

This is a general state library. It does, however, have some Quaker sources for Pennsylvania, including information on the Hicksites and Quaker genealogical material. Research by mail is done on a very limited basis. Please write for further information. The work performed differs for state residents and for those who reside out of state.

Hall of Records, 350 Rowe Boulevard, Annapolis, Maryland 21404

The Hall of Records is the depository for all State of Maryland publications, together with official records from every public official in the state and from each of the counties. It also has a collection of Quaker material. Most of the records are on microfilm, but in some cases original meeting records have been deposited with the Hall of Records, including approximately thirty-five monthly and about ten quarterly meetings. Jurisdictions included in the collection are the Baltimore Yearly Meeting, Stony Run; Baltimore Yearly Meeting, Homewood; Philadelphia Yearly Meetings of the Eastern Shore; and meetings under the Virginia Yearly Meeting. Records of the monthly meetings include registers, marriages, certificates of removal, membership, minutes of the meeting, rough minutes, minutes of women Friends, and minutes of ministry and council.

Mail inquiries will be answered if the research required is confined to the extensive indexes. No family lines will be researched. There is no charge for personal visits, Mondays through Saturdays, 8:30 A.M. to 4:30 P.M.

Indiana Historical Society Library,
140 North Senate Avenue, Indianapolis, Indiana 46204

The Indiana Historical Society Library has published abstracts of Indiana Friends records. There are six parts, with an additional index volume, comprising records which William Wade Hinshaw had copied, together with material found since the time of his work. Willard Heiss, a Quaker and Indiana resident, is the editor of this work, entitled *Encyclopedia of American Quaker Genealogy, Abstracts of the Records of the Society of Friends in Indiana*. These Indiana records are thought of as Volume VII in continuation of Hinshaw's original six volumes. The index volume contains additions, corrections, and comments, and was edited by Roger S. Boone (see Chapter VI).

Library, Indiana University,
Bloomington, Indiana 47401

The main campus of Indiana University at Bloomington has complete files of minutes of the Indiana Yearly Meeting— Orthodox/Guerneyite, and the Western Yearly Meeting—

Orthodox. In addition, the University possesses some of the major periodicals published by Friends, either in the original or on microfilm.

Illinois Historical Survey, University Library, University of Illinois, Urbana, Illinois 61801

The Illinois Historical Survey holds the main body of records for meetings in Illinois, which total eighty-five volumes of 2,200 items. The earliest records begin in 1828. Included are Blue River Quarterly Meeting (1828-1972), Clear Creek Monthly Meeting (1841-1871), the Illinois Yearly Meeting (1875-present), and a group of records for Fox Valley Quarterly Meeting (1952-1962).

Archives/Library, The Ohio Historical Society, 1985 Velma Avenue, Columbus, Ohio 43211

The Ohio Historical Society has a large manuscript collection of Quaker records. Included are minutes of Ohio Yearly Meeting at Short Creek, 1813-1831, and a register of Friends who left England between 1656 and 1787. Original records include minutes, vital records, deeds, indentures, testimonies, correspondence, and other papers of various Ohio meetings and of the New Garden Quarterly Meeting, Fountain City, Indiana. There are notes about the early history of Friends in southeastern Ohio, together with communications with Friends in London, Dublin, Virginia, North Carolina, Pennsylvania, and Indiana.

The Society's microfilm edition of Friends papers includes minutes and proceedings, 1795-1849, from the Baltimore Yearly Meeting's work on Indian affairs, with selected summaries relating to the same from yearly reports, 1795-1862. The original papers were filmed at Friends Boarding School, Barnesville, Ohio and Stony Run Friends Meeting, Baltimore, Maryland.

Photocopies of the records of Stillwater Monthly Meeting, Belmont County, Ohio, may be located through the card file in this library. The original records are in the vault at Friends Boarding School, Barnesville, and are not available to the public.

The Rhode Island Historical Society Library,
   121 Hope Street, Providence, Rhode Island 02906

The Rhode Island Historical Society Library is the home of the New England Yearly Meeting. For information about the holdings, please refer to Chapter VIII.

Newport Historical Society,
   82 Touro Street, Newport, Rhode Island 02840

New England Yearly Meeting records for the seventeenth and eighteenth centuries are located here. Write for information.

Library of Congress,
   Genealogical Reference & Bibliography Division,
   Washington, D. C. 20540

The card catalogue in the Reading Room includes a veritable treasure house of printed material on The Religious Society of Friends. If you are not in the Washington area but happen to be close to a large university library, you will find in the reference room a set of *The National Union Catalog, Pre-1956 Imprints*, published by the American Library Association. These volumes list material held by the Library of Congress, along with the names of libraries across the United States which hold copies of the same material. In Volumes 185 and 186, published in 1972, under the subject heading "Friends, Society of," the following pages list published works: in Volume 185, pages 656-98; in Volume 186, pages 1-88. In Volume 476, published in 1976, under the subject heading "Quakers," you will find lists of transcribed monthly meeting records and certificates of removal. The Quaker meeting material is scattered from page 355 to page 362 among publications by and about a famous cereal company.

CHAPTER X

QUAKER RECORDS
OUTSIDE THE UNITED STATES

I n the event you are successful in tracing your Quaker ancestry to those who immigrated, you may want to continue your search in other countries. There are several locations to which you may write for assistance in tracing forebears. When writing to libraries outside the United States, please include with your request at least two International Reply Coupons (available at any Post Office).

Canada

For those genealogists who have Canadian connections, there are several possibilities.

Archivist, Quaker Collection,
  Pickering College,
  New Market, Ontario, Canada L3Y 4X2

The Canadian Yearly Meeting records are in the Pickering College Quaker Collection. Births, deaths, marriages, and disownments to 1920 are in the Meeting Record Indexes. Write to the archivist for information.

Provincial Archives,
   77 Grenville Street,
   Queen's Park Crescent,
   Toronto, Ontario, Canada M5R 1C7

National Archives,
   Ottawa, Ontario, Canada M54 1C7

The Provincial Archives and the National Archives facilities have microfilms of Canadian Quaker records available for personal research. Early Canadian records are incomplete, but all the surviving records are being indexed.

If you are not close to either of these archives, it is possible to address a request for assistance to the Canadian Friends Historical Association, Canadian Yearly Meeting, 60 Lowther Avenue, Toronto, Ontario, Canada M54 1C7. A basic access fee is charged.

Great Britain

The Religious Society of Friends was a slightly different organization in the British Isles than in the United States. For instance, preparative meetings often met only four times a year. You will also find that policies were different as well. The Society of Genealogists published an excellent guide in 1983 entitled *My Ancestors Were Quakers: How Can I Find More About Them?* by Edward H. Milligan and Malcolm J. Thomas.[11] This small (35-page) booklet is available from that organization (in the fall of 1985 the price was two pounds).

Different conditions for research in the British Isles prevail depending upon whether you are interested in records for England, Wales, Scotland, or Ireland. Original register books of births, marriages, and burials were kept by the individual meetings until 1 July 1837, when civil registration came into effect. The Non-Parochial Registration Act followed shortly thereafter. At that time the register books for England and Wales were surrendered to the Public Record Office and will be found there. However, Scotland and Ireland did not fall under these acts, and their records continued to be held by the monthly or quarterly meetings. As in all research, you are very likely to find that some volumes were lost before the official surrender date of 1840. It is also possible that meeting clerks failed many times to make entries, and you will not find the ancestor you seek.

The Society of Genealogists made digests of each of the meeting registers which had been surrendered to the Public Record Office. One copy was sent to the quarterly meeting with jurisdiction and a second copy was sent to Friends House Library in London.

The following libraries and institutions should be able to assist you. International Reply Coupons should be sent with your written request.

Curator, Historical Library,
   Religious Society of Friends in Ireland,
   6 Eustace Street, Dublin 2, Ireland

At this Friends library, in all probability, there will be a charge for searches you request. It is suggested that inquiries be made about the costs.

Public Record Office, Northern Ireland (PRONI),
   66 Balmoral Avenue,
   Belfast, Northern Ireland BT9 6NY

We suggest you consult Olive C. Goodbody's *Guide to Irish Quaker Records 1654-1860* [12] before writing to this office.

Edinburgh Yearly Meeting
Aberdeen Yearly Meeting

Edinburgh Yearly and Aberdeen Yearly Meetings for church affairs in Scotland were not always held, and registration was sporadic until 1786. But in 1867 digests were prepared of all names in both register books and minute books to 1790. Monthly meeting annual returns from 1867 are included in post-1867 digests. Friends House Library, London, has a copy.

Friends House Library,
   The Religious Society of Friends,
   Euston Road, London NW1 2BJ, England

The holdings at Friends House Library consist of digests of registers of births, marriages, and burials for a number of English and Welsh quarterly and general meetings. In one quarterly meeting for Berkshire and Oxfordshire, birth records begin in 1612, and for the Yorkshire Quarterly Meeting, in 1587. These dates are, of course, before the Society of Friends was organized. In some meetings members carefully recorded data as far back as 1578. So far, we have not been fortunate enough to locate even one of these volumes; in fact, microfilms searched have not been very comprehensive.

In addition, Friends House has minute books for monthly and quarterly meetings in England. They also have journals and accounts of sufferings of early Friends, as well as Quaker manuscripts and four typescript volumes of the "Meeting Records Catalogue." There are additional indexes to help in locating information.

This library charges an hourly rate for you to do your own research. In 1985 this hourly rate was two pounds. If they search for you, it is eight pounds an hour. The cost in dollars will vary depending upon the exchange rate at the time you are working. The library is difficult to use, and it is best to be well prepared with names, dates, and places before visiting. Even with preparation, you will not find the library or the material easy to use.

Society of Genealogists,
   14 Charterhouse Buildings,
   London, EC1M 7BA, England

The library of the Society of Genealogists is extensive. It

has a printed list of the surrendered registers for most Non-Conformist sects before 1837. In addition, you will find indexes of all manner and description with entries from parish registers in the Great Card Index; a document collection; bound family histories; books on schools and universities, professions and apprentices, heraldry, peerages, and pedigrees; and overseas information. They have periodicals, copies of parish registers, heraldic visitations, Boyd's Marriage Index, maps and gazetteers, monumental inscriptions, and a special manuscript collection.

If you are fortunate enough to find your immigrant ancestor in a register book from a meeting in Great Britain, you may want to work at this library to see if you can find that same forebear in parish registers before the beginning of the Quaker movement in the 1650s.

There is a charge for non-members. The society will do work for members, and for others, for a fee; however, members are given priority. We suggest that you write for information before planning a trip. As with the Friends House Library, this library is difficult to use on a first visit, and you will not be accorded personal attention to help you adjust to the differences with our libraries.

Woodbrooke Library, Woodbrooke,
    1046 Bristol Road, Selly Oak,
    Birmingham 29 6LJ, England

Please write for information on their holdings.

A Personal Note

In the fall of 1985 we spent six days attempting to research ancestors in British libraries. It is often difficult to make any progress in these libraries, even if you believe you have excellent data concerning names, locations, dates, etc. The holdings at each library are overwhelming, but the arrangement is strange to Americans and the method of cataloguing difficult to learn rapidly. And in spite of our common language, there are some differences in nomenclature. If you have perhaps a month to spend in Great Britain, working each day at one of these locations, you will make progress. However, with limited time, you may find that the particular record you need is still in a record office in Cardiff, Wales; or you have traveled to York and the register book you need is in North Allerton. The records are probably there (that is the frustrating part of it all), but you are not in the right place for the one you need and do not have time to get to the right place! At the Public Record Office in London the Register of Births for the years 1850-55 was missing from the shelf. No one seemed to know where it could be. This is not meant to discourage you, but "to be fore-warned is to be forearmed!"

CHAPTER **XI**

OTHER NON-QUAKER SOURCES
FOR RECORDS

There is considerable disagreement among Friends libraries about whether Quaker records have been microfilmed. In many cases, individual Quaker repositories have permitted films to be made, but some locations have not permitted this filming to be done. It is therefore necessary to check each repository. (See Chapter VIII for listings of official repositories and a general description of the holdings of each.)

There is one major non-Quaker repository in the United States with a large microfilm collection of Quaker records. This repository is accessible to almost everyone. The Church of Jesus Christ of Latter-day Saints has a large genealogical library in Salt Lake City, Utah. Its branch libraries are located in cities across the country and are listed in the yellow pages of your telephone directory under the "church" listing.

The LDS began a microfilming project in the 1950s which has included many of the monthly meeting records referred to in Chapter VIII. At each branch you will find the Genealogical Library Catalogue (GLC) index on microfiche. This index lists the microfilms which can be ordered and used by you at the branch library. The Quaker records in the GLC index are listed under the heading "Society of Friends." Under that subject heading the listings are arranged by the name of the monthly meeting, then by localities covered by that particular meeting.

The years covered by the microfilm for each meeting are listed, so you will be able to order records for just the time period needed in your search. There is a charge to order each reel of film, and it would be well to plan very carefully before ordering. Usually it takes four to six weeks for film to be delivered to the branch for your use at that library.

The following is a list of the major collections of meeting records filmed by the LDS and available on microfilm through the branch library in your locality, and the locations where these records were filmed:

1. Delaware, Maryland, New Jersey, and Pennsylvania meeting records (Hicksite) under the Philadelphia and Baltimore Yearly Meetings, filmed at Friends Historical Library, Swarthmore College, Swarthmore, Pennsylvania. Also, on seventy-three reels of film is the William Wade Hinshaw Unpublished Index (original at Swarthmore). These are also Hicksite records.

2. Delaware, New Jersey, and Pennsylvania meeting records (Orthodox) under the Philadelphia Yearly Meeting. These records were at one time at the Friends Records Department, Arch Street, Philadelphia, but are now in the Quaker Collection, Haverford College, Haverford, Pennsylvania.

3. Massachusetts, New Hampshire, and Rhode Island records, filmed at the Moses Brown School, Providence, Rhode Island. These records are now in the Quaker Archives, Rhode Island Historical Society Library.

4. New York, New Jersey, Vermont, Massachusetts, Michigan, and Quebec. These records cover those meetings which belonged to the New York Yearly Meeting, and were filmed at the Society of Friends Archives in New York City. They are now at the Haviland Records Room, New York City.

5. Abstracts and transcripts of Pennsylvania, New Jersey, Delaware, Virginia, North Carolina, England, and Scotland records, filmed at the Historical Society of Pennsylvania, in Philadelphia.

6. Records at Wilmington College, Wilmington, Ohio, were filmed on two different occasions. The LDS library has an almost complete collection of these records, which are for meetings under the Ohio Yearly Meeting (see Chapter VIII for a complete account).

7. Handwritten transcripts for Indiana meetings, as well as some of the Ohio meetings, were filmed in Indianapolis, Indiana.

8. England, Scotland, and Wales original meeting records were filmed at the Public Record Office, London, England.

There are three minor record collections which the LDS also filmed:

1. Nantucket Monthly Meeting records. These are original records filmed at the meetinghouse in Rhode Island.

2. Rhode Island meeting records. These records were filmed at the Newport Historical Society. The originals may now be at the Rhode Island Historical Society.

3. North Carolina and Tennessee meeting records. The LDS purchased some films from Guilford College, Greensboro, North Carolina. The Mormons *do not* have the complete collection—only a portion.

Other Sources

There are libraries in many locations which have either microfilms or transcripts of meeting records. For instance:

1. Western Reserve Historical Society, 1095 Euclid Avenue, Cleveland, Ohio 44973, has some records.

2. The Allen County Public Library, Fort Wayne, Indiana, has a good collection of transcribed or abstracted Quaker meeting records. These cover several states and the yearly meetings in those states. This library also has a good collection of Quaker encyclopedias and histories on the open shelves.

The diligent family researcher will find that microfilms, transcripts, and abstracts turn up in unexpected places. Consult the card catalogues or ask the librarians at each repository you visit. Be extremely cautious, however, if you are shown transcripts of records but not microfilms of actual records. As in any abstracted material, Quaker or otherwise, errors can, and do, occur.

CHAPTER XII

PLEASURES AND FRUSTRATIONS

In this chapter we want to give those of you who are searching in Quaker records, or are planning to do so, some words of encouragement, along with a philosophical view of our approach to working in Friends meeting records which contain information on our forebears. As in any endeavor, your work is more pleasurable when the results are positive.

Throughout this book we have emphasized the joys which can be found in studying old Quaker records. Everyone who is interested in genealogy, particularly those with Quaker ancestors, should study the original records of relevant monthly meetings. There is so much to be gained and nothing to be lost, since just a modicum of knowledge of the history of the Friends movement makes the endeavor worthwhile. We realize some of you might feel a tinge of sacrilege in reading church records just for pleasure, but it does happen. The ways of our Quaker ancestors appear strange to us today as we research family names, but there are no punches pulled. The popular expression, "tell it like it is," applies, and along with this phrase comes all the tragedy and pathos, and, yes, even humor, of these people who played a major role in settling this country.

We want to make certain that no one should be intimidated by either the records or, in particular, this book. The purpose in writing it is to assure any literate person, armed with the desire and the stamina, that he or she can learn to use the records. You will find a rhythm developing as you gain experience and confidence, a rhythm which allows you to anticipate moves and actions. Following an entire family for 200 years, just by the records they leave behind, is a thrilling experience. These are not the sterile civil records most of us are forced to use, but rather records with developing patterns which come close to making you feel like a family member. This is an extremely important point. There are not too many church records which allow reconstruction of a lifestyle. Although the stern and rigid nature of the average Quaker makes translation of their records almost an anachronism, with a little imagination we can interpret the entries. A researcher is swept up in the thrill of living along with generation after generation, feeling the joy of birth and the anguish of death, with all the pleasures and problems that lie in between. In short, studying Quaker records can be fun—not just satisfying, but fun. One of the problems is becoming attached to a family, even though that particular family does not constitute your direct ancestors but perhaps represents what you feel is typical of Quakers. You find yourself reading the records of such a family rather than the records of more direct interest. Certainly, this is not always true, but it is not unusual to spend time just reading through the old entries. There simply is no equivalent to Friends records, particularly if the clerk was a meticulous worker. With comprehensive records combined with the usual civil records, our ancestors' stories come to life with color and dimension.

Naturally, there are some disadvantages, as mentioned in the text, and these should be re-emphasized. The first is that the entire experience can be costly unless you are fortunate enough to live close to a Quaker record repository. Even though indexes exist in many instances, they lack the potential that exists in the original records for reaching other families. Because the original records do lack indexes in many cases, a researcher cannot expect to rush into a library and gain any kind of satisfactory information in a few hours. It is a job that requires days, or even weeks. And this is after you become familiar with the various systems of record-keeping. Attacking Quaker records requires diligence and a certain love of old records, but for those equipped to do the work, it is rewarding —almost beyond belief.

It is virtually impossible within the space limitations of this book to list every location where records may be housed. We have attempted to supply a list of the largest and most important of the repositories for The Religious Society of Friends. We have included record sources in the British Isles however, work overseas for the average American is extremely difficult. Consult the Appendix for additional suggestions and aids in locating names of specific meetings.

One more reminder: to start your research, find the proper, or at least the logical, monthly meeting. Without this knowledge, you are helpless. It is not possible to stress this enough. Sometimes this is easy; often it is difficult. But all genealogical research has difficulties, and finding the name of the monthly meeting must be your number one priority, for without this name and location you do not have the key to unlock the vaults of a vast storehouse of records. Use your Quaker librarians and the methods outlined in this book. But FIND THAT MONTHLY MEETING NAME. If you insist on proceeding without it, don't be surprised if you exit empty-handed. The name is the key to your own private record box. We realize this injunction sounds formidable, but we did it, starting with *no* knowledge. This is tantamount to our saying that YOU CAN DO IT.

APPENDIX

A. IMPORTANT DATES
IN THE QUAKER MOVEMENT

With years of establishment of yearly meetings

(To 1900)

1647	George Fox begins his ministry in England
1661	Rhode Island Yearly Meeting
1671	New England Yearly Meeting
1672	Baltimore Yearly Meeting
1673	Virginia Yearly Meeting
1681	Burlington, New Jersey, Yearly Meeting
1681	Philadelphia Yearly Meeting
1685	Burlington and Philadelphia combine
1695	New York Yearly Meeting
1698	North Carolina Yearly Meeting
1812	Ohio Yearly Meeting
1820	Indiana Yearly Meeting
1827	Hicksite Separation
1834	Genesee, New York, Yearly Meeting
1844	Virginia Yearly Meeting laid down (all existing meetings affiliate with Baltimore Yearly Meeting)
1854	Ohio Yearly Meeting separation—Conservative at Barnesville, Ohio; remainder at Damascus, Ohio
1858	Western Yearly Meeting
1863	Iowa Yearly Meeting
1866-67	Canada Yearly Meeting
1872	Kansas Yearly Meeting

1875	Illinois Yearly Meeting
1892-94	Wilmington, Ohio, Yearly Meeting
1893	Oregon Yearly Meeting
1895	California Yearly Meeting

B. TABLE OF CONTENTS

From Volume II of Hinshaw's *Encyclopedia*

CONTENTS

C. RECORDS FROM A HICKSITE MEETING

From Volume II of Hinshaw's *Encyclopedia*

BIRTH AND DEATH RECORDS

ATKINSON
Benjamin d ------1846; m Keslan -----
Ch: Elizabeth d 2- 2-1567
Champion, s Caleb & Sarah, m ----- -----
Ch: Mary Ann
    Rachel
Elizabeth H. -----, 3rd w Champion
Ch: Benjamin H. b 6-12-1832
    Caleb   " 2-16-1834
    Hannah   " 12-31-1835
George W. d 5-21-1866; m Anna K. -----, d 12-14-
    1900
Ch: Miles K.   d 7- 6-1599
    Edith R.
    Budd   " 6-12-1916
    Isaiah   " 12-30-1910
    John   b 3-20-1850
Theodosia d 7-21-1886

BALLINGER
Levi, s David L. & Elizabeth H., b 3-22-1895;
    m Edna H. TOWNSEND, dt Barclay B. & Re-
    becca H., b 8-11-1894
Ch: David R.   b 12-19-1918
    Florence Helen b 11-24-1921

BLACK
William, Jr. & Ann T.
Ch: Thomas Newbole
    Mary T.
    William Henry
    Franklin
    Edwin   d 7- 9-1890
    Sarah Ann
    Caroline   " 12-11-1837
    Emily N.   " 12- 2-1851

BOWKER
Ruth E., dt William & Margaret T. HORNER, b 10-
    5-1902 (or 11-5-1902)

BOWNE
Thomas b 3- 4-1769
Susanna b 1- 1-1776

BRADWAY
Mark d 12-26-1870; m Bulah -----, d 12----1871
Ch: Martha d 10-28-1855

BRIGGS
Yardley & Sarah
Ch: Joshua
    Susan   b 4-17-1837
    Rebecca " 4-17-1837 d 1-26-1843
    John Story b 1-31-1839 (or 1-31-1839)
    Henry S.   " 9-10-1845

BROWN
Julda d 4-14-1877 ae 63y

Lewis W. & Mary L.
Ch: Jacob Leeds b 8- 3-1881
    Ethel G.   " 12-29-1885
Mary L., dt Jacob H. & Margaret W. LEEDS, d 7-
    4-1934 ae 76y bur Harley Cemetery, Camden,
    N. J.
William S. d 10-23-1890 bur Rancocas ae 74; m
    Hulda -----
Ch: Benjamin P.   b 7- 7-1840
    Jonathan P.   " 4-25-1843 d 8- 5-
    1905 bur Bridgeboro, Maine (ae 62)
    Mary   b 4-29-1846
    William H.   " 11- 4-1850
    Lewis W.   " 8-12-1853
    Sarah   " 10- 6-1856
    Anna W.   " 5-17-1862 d 11-12-
    1865

BUNTING
Mary d 5-30-1868

BURNETT
Thomas d 5-26-1900
Abigail T. d 6- 8-----

BUTLER
William B., s Wellington & Ethel B., b 10-1-
    1917

BUZBY
Amos, s Amos & Patience, d 4-22-1868, bur Ran-
    cocas; m Mary -----, d 5-19-1868
Ch: Rebecca D.
    Mary Jane   d 4-11-1915 bur Rancocas (ae
    96y)
    Patience S.

Elgar L. m Nellie STILES, dt Aaron B. & Jane
    E., b 11-11-1887
Ch: Jane Elizabeth b 3-23-1917
    Dorothy L.   " 10-21-1918 d 4- 9-1935
    ae 16y bur Rancocas
Elias S. & Susan A.
Ch: Eliza S.   b 3-10-1850
    Mary W.   " ------1851
    Josephine   d 7-19-1857
    Howard
Josephine d 6-19-1857 bur Rancocas (dt Eliza
    S. & Susan)
Mary d 5-19-1868 bur Rancocas
Phebe W., dt Granville & Phebe W. WOOLMAN,
    d 3-18-1918 ae 69y 8m 22d bur Rancocas
Thomas, s Richard & Mary Ann, d 11-17-1925
    ae 64y 6m bur Rancocas; m Elizabeth
    LEEDS, dt Jacob & Margaret
Ch: Elgar Leeds   b 3-24-1890
    Helen Wilson   " 12-29-1894
    Thomas Harvey " 7-14-1897

CARR
Hannah W. d 6-19-1855
Job d 2-27-1861 bur Rancocas
Ruth d 6-14-1852 (or 6-14-1853)

D. RECORDS FROM AN ORTHODOX MEETING

From Volume II of Hinshaw's *Encyclopedia*

MINUTES AND MARRIAGE RECORDS

ABBOTT

1830, 6,30. George & w, Mary, & minor s, Redman, gct Haddonfield MM

1835, 7,29. Mary & Ann, minors, rocf Greenwich MM, dtd 1835,7,2

1841,10, 6. Martha [Abbotts], dt Samuel & Martha, Salem Co., N. J., m Samuel S. Willits, s Nathan & Judith, Gloucester Co., N. J., at Salem MH, N. J.

1845, 8,27. George gct New Bedford MM, Mass., to m

1846, 2,25. Ruth L. rocf New Bedford MM, dtd 1846,1,22

1846, 5, 6. Samuel, s Samuel & Martha, Salem Co., N. J., m Sarah Wistar, dt Casper & Rebecca, Salem Co., N. J., at Salem MH

1846, 7, 1. Mary dis jas

1872,10, 9. George, s George & Ruth S., Salem Co., N. J., m Elizabeth E. Lippincott, dt Aquila B. & Sarah A., Salem Co., N. J., at Salem MH, N. J.

1872,12, 4. Mary Ann, dt Samuel & Sarah W., Salem Co., N. J., m Josiah Wistar, s Cleaton & Martha, Salem Co., N. J., at Salem MH, N. J.

1874, 1,28. Samuel, Jr. gct WD MM

1876, 6, 2. Samuel, Jr. rocf WD MM, dtd 1876,6, 21

1877, 5, 9. Rebecca W., dt Samuel & Sarah W., Salem Co., N. J., m Chas. W. Warrington, s Henry & Margaret C., Burlington Co., N.J. at Salem MH, N. J.

1878, 8,28. George, Jr. & w, Elizabeth L., & minor ch, Edward L. & George, gct ND MM

1885,12, 2. Henry B. gct Phila. MM

1890, 7, 2. Ruth S. gct Phila. MM

1896,12, 2. Katherine Wistar gct WD MM

ACTON

1828, 4, 4. Hannah dis jH

1828, 5,28. Mary Bassett (late Acton) dis jH

1828, 5,28. Sarah dis jH

1828, 7, 2. Samuel dis jH

1829, 1,28. Richard M., minor, gct Wilmington MM

1829,10,28. Benjamin dis

1829,12, 2. Clement dis jH

1832, 6,27. Richard M. rocf Wilmington MM

1835,10,28. Richard M. dis mcd

1835,12, 2. Hannah (late Mason) dis mcd

1836, 6, 1. Benjamin, Jr. dis jas

1837, 8,30. Richard M. rst

1837, 9,27. Rebecca rst

1837,11, 8. Hannah, dt Benjamin & Sarah, Salem Co., N. J., m Samuel Preston Carpenter, s Wm. & Mary, Salem Co., N. J., at Salem MH

1838,10, 3. Elizabeth W., dt Benjamin & Sarah, Salem Co., N. J., m Franklin Miller, s Wm. F. & Esther, Salem Co., N. J., at Salem MH

1840, 7, 1. Margaret Griscom (late Acton) rpd mcd

1841, 3,31. Clement, Jr. dis jH

1842, 9, 7. Charlotte W., dt Benjamin & Sarah W., Salem Co., N. J., m Richard Wistar, s Clayton & Mary, Salem Co., N. J., at Salem MH, N. J.

1845, 4, 9. Leatitia M., dt Benjamin & Sarah, Salem Co., N. J., m John Wistar, s Clayton & Mary, Salem Co., N. J., at Salem MH, N.J.

1846, 7,29. Caspar W. dis mcd

1865,10,18. Sarah Wyatt, dt Benjamin & Sarah U., Salem, N. J., m Emmer Reeve, s Wm. & Leatitia, Salem Co., N. J., at Salem MH, N.J.

1914, 4,29. George recrq

1915, 4,28. Hannah H. recrq

ALLEN

1828, 4, 4. Sarah N. dis jH

1828, 4,30. Enoch R. dis jH

1829, 7,29. Mary Pancost (late Allen) dis mcd

1830, 3,31. Eliza, minor, gct Woodbury MM

1833, 1,30. Hannah, minor, rocf Woodbury MM, dtd 1833,1,1

1834, 2,28. Sarah Ann, minor, gct Phila. MM

1834, 8,27. Hannah, minor, rocf Woodbury MM, dtd 1834,7,1

1836, 9,28. Samuel, Jr. gct Phila. MM

1836, 9,28. Sarah, minor, gct ND MM

1837, 6,27. Samuel A. dis

1838, 8, 1. Beulah Ann dis jH

1838, 8, 1. Wm., minor, gct Woodbury MM

1838,11,28. Rebecca Inskeep (late Allen) dis mou

1839, 3,27. Richard rpd mcd

1839, 5, 1. Edward gct Haddonfield MM, to m

1839, 8,28. Hannah L. rocf Haddonfield MM, dtd 1839,8,12

1840, 1, 1. Lydia Ware (late Allen) dis mou

1840, 4,29. Joseph dis mcd & jas

1840, 5,27. Franklin, minor, rocf Phila. MM, dtd 1840,3,26

1841,10,27. Sarah Ann rocf Phila. MM, dtd 1841, 8,26

1842, 3,10. David, s Samuel & Mary, Salem Co., N. J., m Sarah Ann Allen, dt Joseph & Hannah, Salem Co., N. J., at Woodstown MH, N. J.

1843, 8,30. Hannah dis jH

1845,10, 6. Hannah, dt Samuel & Mary, Salem Co., N. J., m Francis Bacon, s George & Naomi, Cumberland Co., N. J., at Salem MH

1847, 9,29. Franklin dis jH

1852, 6, 2. Jedediah dis mcd

1853, 3,30. Edward dis

1856, 6,30. Hannah L. & minor ch, Samuel, Sarah & Edward, gct Chester MM, N. J.

1858, 6,30. Jeremiah gct Haddonfield MM

1862,10, 1. Chamles con mou

1868, 9,30. Hannah A. Cowley (late Allen) rpd mou

1875, 4,28. Mary gct Haddonfield MM, N. J.

1875, 4,28. Rebecca gct Haddonfield MM, N. J.

1875, 4,28. Sarah Ann gct Haddonfield MM, N. J.

E. ABBREVIATIONS

(Corresponds with those used in Hinshaw's *Encyclopedia*)

b	born
bur	buried
cert	certificate
ch	child, children
co	chosen overseer(s)
com	complained, complained of
con	condemned
d	died
dec	deceased
dis	disowned, disowned for
dt	daughter(s)
fam	family
form	formerly
gc	granted certificate
gct	granted certificate to
gl	granted letter
h	husband
jas	joined another society
ltm	liberated to marry, left at liberty to marry
m	marry, married, marrying, marriage
mbr	member
mbrp	membership
mcd	married contrary to discipline
MH	meeting house
MM	monthly meeting

mos	married out of society
mou	married out of unity
mtg	meeting
prc	produced a certificate
prcf	produced a certificate from
QM	quarterly meeting
rec	receive, received
recrq	received by request
relfc	released from care for
relrq	released by request
rem	remove, removed
rm	reported married
rmt	reported married to
roc	received on certificate
rocf	received on certificate from
rol	received on letter
rolf	received on letter from
rpd	reported
rq	request, requests, requested
rqc	requested certificate
rqct	requested certificate to
rqcuc	requested to come under care (of mtg)
rst	reinstate, reinstated
s	son(s)
uc	under care (of mtg)
w	wife
YM	yearly meeting

F. MAPS OF MEETING LOCATIONS

Throughout this book we have emphasized the importance of finding the monthly meeting, or meetings, your ancestors attended before you can find any substantive data. In fact, Chapter VI is devoted to the subject of how to find monthly meetings. In that chapter we state that maps included in the Appendix might help you to find the proper meeting (for any Pennsylvania ancestors). Three of these follow: the Philadelphia Yearly Meeting, the Philadelphia Quarterly Meeting, and the Concord Quarterly Meeting. Although these maps are taken from Ezra Michener's *Retrospect of Early Quakerism* (Philadelphia, 1860), almost all Quaker libraries have similar maps, but perhaps not in this exact format. These maps are shown only as examples of the types of aids available if you seek such help. Notice the geographical area covered; it is relatively small. But if you have an approximate location for your ancestor, maps of this general type can be invaluable.

Let us assume you know your forebears came from the general area of Chester County near Philadelphia; you know also that the Friends' organization is almost invariably built around a particular yearly meeting. You can find the quarterly meetings on the Philadelphia Yearly Meeting map, along with their relative positions and distances from Philadelphia. Then, after selecting the most likely quarterly meeting, go to that quarterly meeting map to find the juxtaposition of monthly meetings reporting to that particular quarterly. By narrowing your choices of the logical monthly meetings to perhaps two at the beginning, you can search those records with much more assurance that you will find the correct names. We have used this technique many times and have usually been successful. When you are faced with dozens of monthly meetings, any technique

114

to narrow your choices to a relative few is welcome. A combination of geography and logic is often the answer. Remember also that the librarian where you are working is your best friend. Do not hesitate to ask questions, because the same procedure can be used for other states.

We have included only two of the quarterly maps under the Philadelphia Yearly Meeting to illustrate the use of such maps. The relative positions and distances of the meetings shown on the three maps are fairly accurate. Dotted lines indicate where quarterly meetings were held; the solid black lines connect several meetings which compose each monthly meeting. In addition, the open circles indicate a meeting for worship or a preparative meeting; the solid circles indicate a monthly meeting; the open circles with an inner circle indicate a quarterly meeting; and the crosses within circles show where a former meeting has been discontinued.

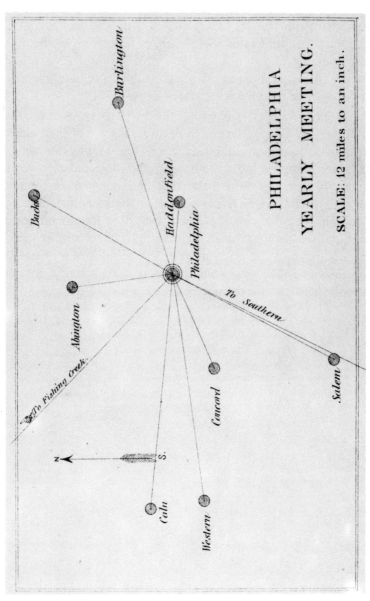

PHILADELPHIA
YEARLY MEETING.

SCALE: 12 miles to an inch.

From Ezra Michener's *Retrospect of Early Quakerism* (Phila., 1860)

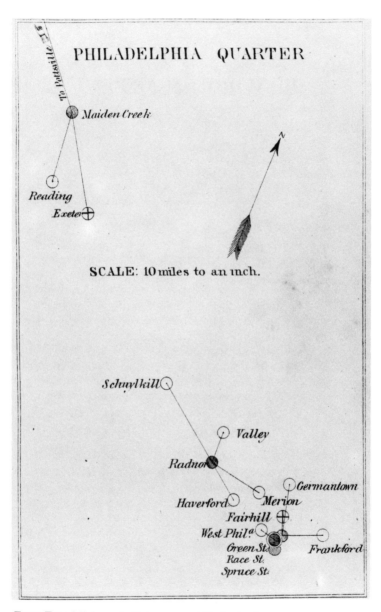

PHILADELPHIA QUARTER

To Pottsville Ps.

Maiden Creek

Reading

Exeter

SCALE: 10 miles to an inch.

Schuylkill

Valley

Radnor

Haverford

Merion

Germantown

Fairhill

West Phil.ᵃ

Green St.

Race St.

Spruce St.

Frankford

From Ezra Michener's *Retrospect of Early Quakerism* (Phila., 1860)

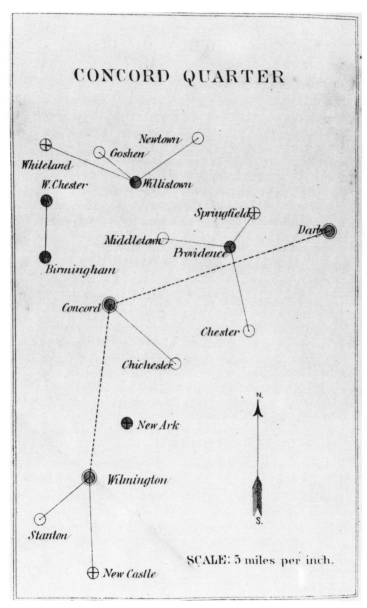

CONCORD QUARTER

Newtown
Goshen
Whiteland
W.Chester Willistown
Springfield
Middletown Darb
Providence
Birmingham
Concord Chester
Chichester
N.
New Ark
Wilmington
S.
Stanton
SCALE: 5 miles per inch.
New Castle

From Ezra Michener's *Retrospect of Early Quakerism* (Phila., 1860)

G. PRESENT-DAY YEARLY MEETINGS
From FWCC 1985-1986 Friends Directory
(Friends World Committee for Consultation)

KEY TO MEETINGS OF THE AMERICAS
AND THEIR AFFILIATIONS
AFFILIATIONS OF YEARLY MEETINGS

C **CONSERVATIVE**, three yearly meetings. Unprogrammed worship.
No appointed pastors or paid staff.

E **EVANGELICAL FRIENDS ALLIANCE**, four yearly meetings
especially concerned for church growth and Christian mission.
Programmed worship. Appointed pastors in all meetings or
churches.

F **FRIENDS UNITED MEETING**, yearly meetings in North America, and
in the Caribbean and Africa. Most local meetings use
programmed worship and appointed pastoral leadership.

G **FRIENDS GENERAL CONFERENCE**, includes eleven yearly meetings
in North America. Five of these are also affiliated with FUM.
Most local meetings use unprogrammed worship, without
appointed pastors.

I **"INDEPENDENT"**, a yearly meeting which has adopted none of the
affiliations described above. Practices in worship and
leadership vary.

MEETINGS WITH NO YEARLY MEETING AFFILIATION

UN Local Meeting with no formal link to a Yearly Meeting

FG Meeting for Worship which reports to Friends General Conference

FW Meeting for Worship which reports to Friends World Committee for
Consultation

YEARLY MEETINGS
(in USA unless otherwise indicated)

Note: The initial to the left indicates the YM designation used in the text of
the *Directory*.

(AL) **ALASKA YM OF FRIENDS CHURCH (I),** Walter E. Outwater,
Supt., Box 687, Kotzebue, AK 99752 Tel: 907-442-3906

(B) **BALTIMORE YM OF FRIENDS (F & G),** Thomas H. Jeavons, Ex.
Sec., 17100 Quaker Lane, Sandy Spring, MD 20860 Tel:
301-774-7663

119

(BV) **BOLIVIA NATIONAL CHURCH OF EVANGELICAL FRIENDS**
(I), Humberto Gutierrez, Correo 8385, Max Paredes #776, La
Paz, Bolivia

(CA) **CALIFORNIA YM OF FRIENDS CHURCH (F)**, Charles
Mylander, Supt., P.O. Box 1607, Whittier, CA 90609 Tel:
213-947-2883

(CN) **CANADIAN YM, RELIGIOUS SOCIETY OF FRIENDS (F & G)**,
Frank Miles, Gen. Sec., 60 Lowther Ave., Toronto, Ont. M5R
1C7, Canada Tel: 416-922-2632

(CF) **CENTRAL ALASKAN FRIENDS CONFERENCE (G)**, c/o Mike
Monroe, 5240 E 42nd, Anchorage, AK 99507 Tel:
907-333-2015

(CB) **CENTRAL AMERICA YM OF EVANGELICAL FRIENDS
CHURCHES (I)**, Mario Rolando Lopez Espana, Supt.,
Apartado 8, Chiquimula, Guatemala, CA Tel: 420-229

(C) **CENTRAL YM OF FRIENDS CHURCH (I)**, Ollie McCune, Supt.,
Rte. 1, Box 226, Alexandria, IN 46001 Tel: 317-724-7083

(CB) **CUBA YM (F)**, Ernesto Gurri, Clerk, Calixto Garcia 69, Gibrara,
Holguin, Cuba

(EF) **EVANGELICAL FRIENDS CHURCH, EASTERN REGION (E)**,
Robert Hess, Gen. Supt., 1201 30th St., NW, Canton, OH
44709 Tel: 216-493-1660

(HN) **HONDURAS YM (I)**, Juan Garcia, Supt., Iglesia Evangelica
Amigos, San Marcos, Ocotepeque, Honduras, C.A. Tel:
62-02-86

(IL) **ILLINOIS YM OF FRIENDS (G)**, Alice Walton, Clerk, 1421
Northwoods Dr., Deerfield, IL 60015 Tel: 312-945-1774

(IN) **INDIANA YM OF FRIENDS (F)**, Richard Newby, Clerk, 418 W
Adams St., Muncie, IN 47305 Tel: 317-288-5680

(IM) **INTERMOUNTAIN YM, RELIGIOUS SOCIETY OF FRIENDS**
(I), Anne White, Clerk, Sunshine Canyon, Boulder, CO 80302
Tel: 303-444-0169

(IC) **IOWA YM OF FRIENDS (C)**, John Griffith, Clerk, 5745 Charlotte
Ave., Kansas City, MO 64110 Tel: 816-444-2543

(IF) **IOWA YM OF FRIENDS (F)**, Stephen Main, Gen. Supt., Box 703,
Oskaloosa, IA 52577 Tel: 515-673-9717

(JA) **JAMAICA YM OF FRIENDS (F)**, Nelly Malloy, Clerk,
11 Caledonia Ave., Kingston 8, Jamaica, WI

(LE) **LAKE ERIE YM, RELIGIOUS SOCIETY OF FRIENDS (G)**, Isabel
N. Bliss, Clerk, 7700 Clark's Lake Rd., Chelsea, MI 48118
Tel: 313-475-9976

(MA) **MID-AMERICA YM OF FRIENDS (E)**, Maurice A. Roberts,
Supt., 2018 Maple, Wichita, KS 67213 Tel: 316-267-0391

(NB) **NEBRASKA YM OF FRIENDS (F)**, Kay Mesner, Clerk, Rte. 1, Box
65, Central City, NE 68826 Tel: 308-946-3669

(NE) **NEW ENGLAND YM OF FRIENDS (F & G)**, Thomas Ewell, Fld.
Sec., P.O. Box 2432, S Portland, ME 04106 Tel: 207-799-6320

(NY) **NEW YORK YM, RELIGIOUS SOCIETY OF FRIENDS (F & G)**,
Joseph A. Vlaskamp, Gen. Sec., 15 Rutherford Place, New
York, NY 10003 Tel: 212-673-5750

(NC) **NORTH CAROLINA YM OF FRIENDS (C)**, Louise B. Wilson,
Clerk, 113 Pinewood Rd., Virginia Beach, VA 23451
Tel: 804-428-7853

(NF) **NORTH CAROLINA YM, RELIGIOUS SOCIETY OF FRIENDS
(F)**, Billy M. Britt, Supt., 903 New Garden Rd., Greensboro,
NC 27410 Tel: 919-292-6957

(NP) **NORTH PACIFIC YM (I)**, Barbara Janoe, Clerk, Rte. 1, Box 403,
Terrebonne, OR 97760 Tel: 503-584-5854

(N) **NORTHERN YM (G)**, Perry-O Sliwa, RR 2, Box 104, Decorah, IA
52101 Tel: 319-382-3922

(NW) **NORTHWEST YM OF FRIENDS CHURCH (E)**, Jack L.
Willcuts, Gen. Supt., P.O. Box 190, Newberg, OR 97132
Tel: 503-538-9419

(OV) **OHIO VALLEY YM (G)**, Barbara Hill, Clerk, 6921 Stonington Rd.,
Cincinnati, OH 45230 Tel: 513-232-5348

(OC) **OHIO YM OF FRIENDS (C)**, William L. Cope, Clerk, 44550 State
Rt. 517, Columbiana, OH 44408 Tel: 216-457-2949

(PA) **PACIFIC YM, RELIGIOUS SOCIETY OF FRIENDS (I)**, Robert S.
Vogel, Clerk, 1678 Casitas Ave., Pasadena, CA 91103
Tel: 707-538-3159

(PE) **PERUVIAN FRIENDS NATIONAL CHURCH (I)**, Ignacio
Mamani, Supt, Giron San Sebastian #205 & #207, Ylave, Peru

(PH) **PHILADELPHIA YM, RELIGIOUS SOCIETY OF FRIENDS (G)**,
Samuel D. Caldwell, Gen. Sec., 1515 Cherry St., Philadelphia,
PA 19102 Tel: 215-241-7210

(R) **ROCKY MOUNTAIN YM OF FRIENDS CHURCH (E),** Jack C. Rea, Gen. Sup., 29 N Garland Ave., Colorado Springs, CO 80909 Tel: 303-636-2729

(SC) **SOUTH CENTRAL YM OF FRIENDS (G),** Yvonne Boeger, Clerk, 3701 Garnet St., Houston, TX 77005 Tel: 713-664-8467

(SE) **SOUTHEASTERN YM, RELIGIOUS SOCIETY OF FRIENDS (F & G),** Gene E. Beardsley, Sec., Rt. 3, Box 108F, Gainesville, FL 32606 Tel: 904-462-3201

(SA) **SOUTHERN APPALACHIAN YM & ASSOCIATION (G),** Beth Stafford, Clerk, 3135 Long Blvd., Nashville, TN 37203 Tel: 615-292-2494

(W) **WESTERN YM OF FRIENDS CHURCH (F),** Robert E. Garris, Gen. Supt., 8 Michael Dr., Plainfield, IN 46168 Tel: 317-839-2789

(WL) **WILMINGTON YM, RELIGIOUS SOCIETY OF FRIENDS (F),** Robert E. Beck, Ex. Sec., Wilmington College, Box 1194, Wilmington, OH 45177 Tel: 513-382-2491

Date and location of annual sessions are provided in the *Calendar of Yearly Meetings* published each year in January by the World Office of FWCC. Copies of this *Calendar* are free on request by sending a self-addressed, stamped envelope to any office of Friends World Committee for Consultation.

NOTES

1. Janet Whitney, "The Apprenticeship of George Fox," *Journal of the Friends Historical Society* 51 (1965):434.

2. Stephen B. Weeks, *Southern Quakers and Slavery,* Johns Hopkins University Studies in Historical and Political Science, no. 15 (Baltimore, 1896).

3. Walter Lee Sheppard, Jr., comp. and ed., *Passengers and Ships Prior To 1684* (Baltimore: Genealogical Publishing Co., 1970), vol. I, *Penn's Colony*; George E. McCracken, *The Welcome Claimants Proved, Disproved and Doubtful* (Baltimore: Genealogical Publishing Co., 1970), vol. II, *Penn's Colony.*

4. Arnold Lloyd, *Quaker Social History, 1669-1738* (London: Longmans, Green and Co., 1948), p. 2.

5. Ibid., pp. 1-2.

6. *Hopewell Friends History, 1734-1934, Frederick County, Virginia* (Joint Committee of Hopewell Friends, 1936; reprint, Baltimore: Genealogical Publishing Co., 1975).

7. Weeks, *Southern Quakers and Slavery,* pp. 246-47.

8. James L. Burke and Donald E. Bensch, *Mount Pleasant and the Early Quakers of Ohio* (Columbus, Ohio: The Ohio Historical Society, 1975).

9. Elizabeth H. Moger, "Records of New York Yearly Meeting of The Society of Friends and the Haviland Records Room, New York City," *Tree Talks* (Publication of the Central New York Genealogical Society) 25, no. 1 (1985):3.

10. Ibid., pp. 3-4.

11. Edward H. Milligan and Malcolm J. Thomas, *My Ancestors Were Quakers: How Can I Find More About Them?* (London: The Society of Genealogists, 1983).

12. Olive C. Goodbody, *Guide to Irish Quaker Records, 1654-1860* (Dublin: Stationery Office, 1967).

GLOSSARY

Acknowledgment. A formal acknowledgment by a member, in writing, of having acted in a manner contrary to discipline.

Certificate. Generally, given to a member for movement between meetings. This included those given to ministers by their home meeting for travel to other locations and which were returned to the home meeting when the ministry was completed.

Disownment. When a member of the Society of Friends acted in a manner contrary to discipline, that member was visited by a committee appointed by the meeting. If the member failed to acknowledge fault after visitation by the committee, then the member was disowned by the Society and could not be reinstated until acknowledgment of fault was made.

Laid Down. Term for the official discontinuance of a meeting.

Marriage Certificate. Document which was the official record that a marriage had taken place. No minister or other person officially performed a ceremony. Other papers which may be found as a part of the marriage process are: a record from the respective meetings, if appropriate, which stated the parties in question were of good character and free of any marriage commitments; a record of the parental consent to the marriage (if the parents were living); a letter from the parents giving consent to the marriage. This process may cover a period of more than one month.

Meetings

Indulged Meeting. A meeting for worship only. Set up by a monthly meeting when a preparative meeting was impractical.

Men's and Women's Meetings. In the early years, separate meetings for business were held at the same location. Meetings for worship were held in the same room, men sitting on one side of the room, women on the other. Women's meetings were concerned only with the affairs of women in the meeting and records were kept of each meeting. In matters of discipline, and occasionally at other times, the two clerks would both sign the minute records. Matters of interest to both men and women were handled by small committees from each meeting, since they met at the same time and location but in separate rooms. Representatives, in pairs, could be sent to the other meeting when necessary. About 1880 separate men's and women's meetings began to disappear.

Monthly Meeting. The main, and genealogically important, unit of the Society of Friends. Membership included members from all the indulged and preparative meetings under the jurisdiction of the monthly meeting. All registers of the subordinate meetings, and all business minutes, were kept by the monthly meeting. Final decisions in all matters were made in the monthly meeting. All members within its jurisdiction were expected to attend the business meetings.

Particular Meeting. May have several meanings. It could be a worship meeting under a monthly meeting. Occasionally, it was a meeting of ministering Friends (especially in the early years), or it could distinguish a monthly from a quarterly meeting of the same name.

Preparative Meeting. Officially authorized by Philadelphia Yearly Meeting in 1698. As the term was originally used, it indicated a committee appointed by the monthly meeting for the "preparation" of an agenda to be presented to the monthly meeting for action. When a meeting for worship was permitted, but not officially set-up as a monthly meeting, a committee was appointed to "oversee" the affairs of the meeting for worship. Complaints or business matters were first given to this committee for preparation in proper form and, later, presentation to the monthly meeting. Later, the entire meeting was included in the term "preparative," not just the committee. The preparative meetings kept records, and their actions were subject to the decisions of the appropriate monthly meeting; in addition, the minutes of preparative meetings had to be approved by that monthly meeting.

Quarterly Meeting. Business meetings composed of one or more monthly meetings. Early, monthly meetings sometimes called every third meeting a "quarterly" meeting. Later, several monthly meetings united at the time of the third meeting. Duties of the quarterly meeting were: to set-up new monthly meetings; to combine meetings when necessary; to consider matters brought to them from monthly meetings; to give advice and admonition for the general good of the entire membership.

Worship, Meeting for. These meetings were usually held on First-days, and sometimes one was held during the week. No preacher or leader was used, as the oral ministry of any member could be given. Sometimes the entire meeting was held in a silent communion of worship and the waiting upon God for the leading of His Spirit.

Yearly Meeting. Business meetings composed of several quarterly meetings. The entire membership was supposed to attend. Prominent members of the several meetings usually did attend, although they were not elected nor were they delegates to the yearly meeting. However, certain members of quarterly and monthly meetings were designated to attend in order to facilitate the business of their respective meetings.

Memorial. A written tribute to commemorate the name of an outstanding member who had recently died. Prepared by the Overseers, by individuals, or by a designated committee. As listed in Friends' records, memorials are a collection of these tributes and are sometimes found in published form.

Minister. Both men and women in the early years were recognized and recorded by special action of the monthly and quarterly meetings as "having a gift for the ministry." A Friends minister had the same legal status as ordained ministers of other denominations.

Overseers. Two or more men or women appointed by each monthly meeting to have pastoral care of the members. They reported to the monthly meeting. At times, they met with the ministers and elders; any records kept by the Overseers are found with records of the ministers and elders.

Removal. A certificate, or a record, of persons who moved to the jurisdiction of another meeting. The certificate stated that the person or family in question was in good standing with the meeting issuing the certificate.

Set-Off. Term used when a new meeting is formed from the division of another meeting.

Set-Up. Term used when a new meeting was established by a superior meeting, e.g. when a quarterly meeting established a new monthly meeting, or a yearly meeting set up a new quarterly meeting.

Testimony. A belief or conviction of Friends in general, and the promotion of that belief or conviction.

BIBLIOGRAPHY

Bacon, Margaret H. *The Quiet Rebels: The Story of the Quakers in America.* New York: Basic Books, 1969.

A good general introduction to the Quaker movement.

Bell, James P. *Our Quaker Friends of Ye Olden Time.* 1905. Reprint. Baltimore: Genealogical Publishing Co., 1976.

A transcript of minute books of Cedar Creek Meeting, Hanover County, and the South River Meeting, Campbell County, Virginia.

Brinton, Howard H. *Friends for 300 Years.* 1952. Reprint. Wallingford, PA: Pendle Hill & Philadelphia Yearly Meeting, 1965.

A history of the Society of Friends and its beliefs since George Fox began the movement.

Bronner, Edwin B. *William Penn's Holy Experiment: The Founders of Pennsylvania 1681-1701.* New York: Temple University Publications, Columbia University Press, 1962.

A study of the first two decades of Quakers in Pennsylvania.

Brown, Douglas Summers. *A History of Lynchburg's Pioneer Quakers and Their Meeting House 1754-1936.* Lynchburg, VA: J. P. Bell, 1936.

Browning, Charles H. *Welsh Settlement of Pennsylvania.* 1912. Reprint. Baltimore: Genealogical Publishing Co., 1967.

Burke, James L. and Gensch, Donald E. *Mount Pleasant and the Early Quakers of Ohio.* Columbus: The Ohio Historical Society, 1975.

Carroll, Kenneth L. *Quakerism on the Eastern Shore.* Baltimore: Maryland Historical Society, 1970.

The early history of Baltimore Yearly Meeting, particularly the Chesapeake Bay area.

—*Three Hundred Years and More of Third Haven Quakerism.* Easton, MD: The Queen Anne Press; Baltimore: Reese Press, 1984.

History of a Talbot County, Maryland, meeting established in the mid-1600s.

A Collection of Memorials Concerning Divers Deceased Ministers and Others of the People Called Quakers. Philadelphia: Joseph Crukshank, Printer, 1787.

This volume is written for "Pennsylvania, New Jersey, and Parts adjacent, from nearly the first Settlement thereof to the Year 1787." Similar volumes of memorials are found in many Quaker libraries.

Cope, Gilbert. *Genealogy of Dunwoody and Hood Families, and Collateral Branches.* Minneapolis: Tribune Printing, 1899.

—*Genealogy of the Baily Family of Bromham, Wiltshire, England.* Lancaster, PA: Wickersham Printing, 1912.

—*Genealogy of the Darlington Family.* West Chester, PA: 1900.

—*Genealogy of the Dutton Family of Pennsylvania.* West Chester, PA: 1871.

—*Genealogy of the Sharpless Family.* Philadelphia: 1887.

—*Genealogy of the Smedley Family.* Lancaster, PA: Wickersham Printing, 1901.

—*Historic Homes and Institutions and Genealogical and Personal Memoirs of Chester and Delaware Counties, Pennsylvania.* New York and Chicago: Lewis Publishing Co., 1904.

—and Futhey, John Smith. *History of Chester County, Pennsylvania, with Genealogical and Biographical Sketches.* Philadelphia: L. H. Everts, 1881.

Davis, Eileen and Ireton, Judith. *Quaker Records of the Miami Valley of Ohio.* Owensboro, KY: Cook-McDowell Publications, 1981.

Elliott, Errol T. *Quakers on the American Frontier.* Richmond, IN: Friends United Press, 1969.

An overview of the westward movement of Friends.

Eustace, P. Beryl and Goodbody, Olive C. *Quaker Records, Dublin: Abstracts of Wills.* Dublin, Ireland: Stationery Office, 1957.

Fawcett, Thomas H. "Quaker Migration from Pennsylvania and New Jersey to Hopewell Monthly Meeting, 1732-1759." *Bulletin of Friends Historical Association* 26, no. 2 (Autumn 1937): 102-108.

Friends, Society of. *Two Hundred and Fifty Years of Quakerism at Birmingham 1690-1940, Birmingham, Pennsylvania.* West Chester, PA, 1940.

Frost, Josephine C.

Mrs. Frost transcribed and published records of many meetings in New York State. She was a researcher whose prodigious output was printed in New York between 1900 and 1940 and includes genealogies, some of which may contain Quaker names.

Frost, J. William. *The Quaker Family in Colonial America: A Portrait of the Society of Friends.* New York: St. Martin's Press, 1973.

Glenn, Thomas Allen. *Merion in the Welsh Tract.* 1896. Reprint. Baltimore: Genealogical Publishing Co., 1970.

—*Welsh Founders of Pennsylvania.* 2 vols. 1911-13. Reprint. Baltimore: Genealogical Publishing Co., 1970.

Goodbody, Olive C. *Guide to Irish Quaker Records, 1654-1860.* Dublin: Stationery Office, for the Irish Manuscripts Commission, 1967.

Grubb, Isabel. *Quakers in Ireland 1654-1900.* London: Swarthmore Press, 1927.

Hamm, Thomas D. and Heiss, Willard C. *Quaker Genealogies, A Selected List of Books.* Boston: New England Historic Genealogical Society, 1986.

Haverford College, Pennsylvania. Magill Library. *Dictionary of Quaker Biography*. Typescript. The Quaker Collection.

Quaker Necrology. 2 vols. Boston: G. K. Hall, 1961.

An index of names from Quaker publications which listed deaths of members living in Pennsylvania, New Jersey, and Delaware, together with some items from Maryland, New York, Ohio, and Indiana, from 1828 to 1960.

Heiss, Willard C., ed. *Encyclopedia of American Quaker Genealogy, Abstracts of Records of the Society of Friends in Indiana*. Vol VII. Indianapolis: Indiana Historical Society, 1962-77.

Issued in six parts, plus an index volume, this includes records copied by Heiss, together with material found since Hinshaw's work.

—*Guide to Research in Quaker Records in the Midwest*. Indianapolis: John Woolman Press, 1962.

—"A List of All the Friends Meetings That Exist or Ever Have Existed in Indiana 1807-1955." Indianapolis: 1959. Rev. 1986. Typescript.

Hill, Thomas C. "Quaker Meetings in Southwest Ohio." Cincinnati, 1986. Typescript.

The Quaker meetings listed in this catalogue include meetings under Wilmington Yearly and Ohio Valley Yearly Meetings. The list is on file in the Quaker Collection, Haverford College, Haverford, Pennsylvania, and at the Friends Historical Library, Swarthmore College, Swarthmore, Pennsylvania. It may also be found in the Quaker libraries at Wilmington and Malone Colleges in Ohio.

Hinshaw, Seth B. *The Carolina Quaker Experience*. Greensboro: North Carolina Friends Historical Society, North Carolina Yearly Meeting, 1984.

—and Hinshaw, Mary Edith, eds. *Carolina Quakers*. Greensboro: North Carolina Yearly Meeting, 1972.

Hinshaw, William Wade. *An Encyclopedia of American Quaker Genealogy.* 6 vols. Ann Arbor, MI: Edwards Bros., 1936-50. Reprint. Baltimore: Genealogical Publishing Co., 1969-73.

Abstracted Quaker records for North and South Carolina, Georgia, Tennessee, New Jersey, Pennsylvania, New York City and Long Island, southwestern Pennsylvania, Ohio, Virginia, and one meeting in Michigan.

Hopewell Friends Joint Committee. *Hopewell Friends History, 1734-1934, Frederick County, Virginia.* 1936. Reprint. Baltimore: Genealogical Publishing Co., 1975.

Jacobsen, Phebe R. *Quaker Records in Maryland.* Annapolis: The Hall of Records Commission, State of Maryland, 1966.

James, Sydney V. *A People Among Peoples: Quaker Benevolence in Eighteenth-Century America.* Cambridge: Harvard University Press, 1963.

Information on Quakers in all of the colonies is included in this book. While no meeting records are given, there are individuals named.

Jones, Rufus M. *The Quakers in the American Colonies.* 1911. Reprint. New York: W. W. Norton, 1966.

Kelly, J. Reaney. *Quakers in the Founding of Anne Arundel County, Maryland.* Baltimore: Maryland Historical Society, 1963.

Lloyd, Arnold. *Quaker Social History, 1669-1738.* London: Longmans, Green and Co., 1948.

Lloyd, Howard Williams. *Lloyd Manuscripts.* Lancaster, PA: New Era Printing, 1912.

Genealogies of a number of Quaker families.

Medlin, William F. *Quaker Families of South Carolina and Georgia.* Columbia, SC: Ben Franklin Press, 1982.

Mendenhall, William and Mendenhall, Edward. *History, Correspondence and Pedigrees of the Mendenhalls of England, the United States and Africa.* 1865. Reprint. Greenville, OH: Charles R. Kemble Press, 1912.

Michener, Ezra. *A Retrospect of Early Quakerism, Being Extracts from the Records of Philadelphia Yearly Meeting.* Philadelphia: T. Ellwood Zell, 1860.

These records are from the meetings under the Philadelphia Yearly Meeting from 1681.

Milligan, Edward H. and Thomas, Malcolm J. *My Ancestors Were Quakers: How Can I Find More About Them?* London: The Society of Genealogists, 1983.

Moore, John M., ed. *Friends in the Delaware Valley.* Philadelphia: Friends Historical Society, 1981.

Mote, Luke Smith. *Early Settlement of Friends in the Miami Valley,* ed. Willard Heiss. Indianapolis: John Woolman Press, 1961.

Myers, Albert Cook. *Immigration of the Irish Quakers into Pennsylvania 1682-1750. With Their Early History in Ireland.* 1902. Reprint. Baltimore: Genealogical Publishing Co., 1969.

—*Quaker Arrivals at Philadelphia 1682-1750.* 1902. Reprint. Baltimore: Genealogical Publishing Co., 1969.

A list of certificates of removal received at Philadelphia Monthly Meeting of Friends.

National Genealogical Society. *General Aids to Genealogical Research.* Washington, DC, 1962.

Contains an article by Frederick B. Tolles listing all the meeting records found in the William Wade Hinshaw Index to Quaker Meeting Records in the Friends Historical Library, Swarthmore College, Swarthmore, Pennsylvania.

New York. Works Progress Administration. *Inventory of Church Archives, Society of Friends.* New York, 1940.

A survey prepared under the Works Progress Administration, Federal Works Administration.

Newlin, Algie I. *Friends "At the Spring": A History of Spring Monthly Meeting.* Greensboro, NC: North Carolina Friends Historical Society, 1984.

The fourth in a series of meeting histories sponsored by the North Carolina Friends Historical Society, the Yearly Meeting, and the local meeting.

—*The Newlin Family: Ancestors and Descendants of John and Mary Pyle Newlin.* With Harvey Newlin. Greensboro, NC: Algie I. Newlin, 1965.

Passmore, John Andrew Moore. *Ancestors and Descendants of Andrew Moore, 1612-1897.* 2 vols. Philadelphia, 1897.

Pennsylvania Historical Survey. *Inventory of Church Archives, Society of Friends in Pennsylvania.* Philadelphia: Friends Historical Association, 1941.

A survey prepared under the Works Progress Administration, Federal Works Administration.

(Pennsylvania Magazine of History and Biography.) Genealogies of Pennsylvania Families. Intro. by Milton Rubincam. Baltimore: Genealogical Publishing Co., 1981.

Articles reprinted from the Pennsylvania Magazine of History and Biography *about families in Pennsylvania and the Delaware Valley.*

Publications of the Genealogical Society of Pennsylvania. Lancaster and Philadelphia, 1895-

Philadelphia Monthly Meeting records from 1682 are found in the first fifteen volumes of this series. Included are births, deaths, marriages, certificates of removal, and committee actions. There are also lists of wills found at Philadelphia. Later volumes may have occasional Quaker information. In 1948 the name of this journal was changed to the Pennsylvania Genealogical Magazine.

Punshon, John. *Portrait in Grey, A Short History of the Quakers.* London: Quaker Home Service, 1984.

This is a good short history of the Quaker movement from its beginnings in England, written from the perspective of an Englishman.

Rhode Island. Works Progress Administration. *Inventory of Church Archives, Society of Friends.* Providence, 1939.

A survey prepared under the Works Progress Administration, Federal Works Administration.

Roberts, Clarence V. *Early Friends Families of Upper Bucks. With Some Account of Their Descendants.* 1925. Reprint. Genealogical Publishing Co., 1975.

Historical and genealogical information about the early Quaker settlers in upper Bucks County, Pennsylvania.

Russell, Elbert. *The History of Quakerism.* New York: Macmillan, 1942.

A very good history, particularly the author's explanation of the separations which took place in America in the Religious Society of Friends.

Thomas, Allen C. *A History of the Friends in America.* Philadelphia: Winston, 1930.

Tolles, Frederick B. *Meeting House and Counting House: The Quaker Merchants of Colonial Philadelphia 1682-1763.* 1948. Reprint. New York: Norton Press, 1963.

The Quaker upper class in Philadelphia.

Trueblood, D. Elton. *The People Called Quakers.* 1966. Reprint. Richmond, IN: Friends United Press, 1971.

Weeks, Stephen B. *Southern Quakers and Slavery.* Baltimore: Johns Hopkins University Press, 1896.

Contains surnames found in southern meetings and the names of families who removed to Ohio and westward.

Welcome Society of Pennsylvania. *Penn's Colony: Genealogical and Historical Materials Relating to the Settlement of Pennsylvania.* 2 vols. Baltimore: Genealogical Publishing Co., 1970.

Volume I, ed. Walter Lee Sheppard, Jr., lists passengers and ships prior to 1684, and Volume II, by George E. McCracken, has information about the claimants of the Welcome *and discusses those who have been "proved, disproved and doubtful."*

White, Miles Jr. *Early Quaker Records in Virginia.* 1902-03. Reprint. Baltimore: Genealogical Publishing Co., 1979.

Birth, death, and marriage records of Nansemond and Isle of Wight counties, beginning in 1673.

"FAMILY TREE" OF AMERICAN YEARLY MEETINGS

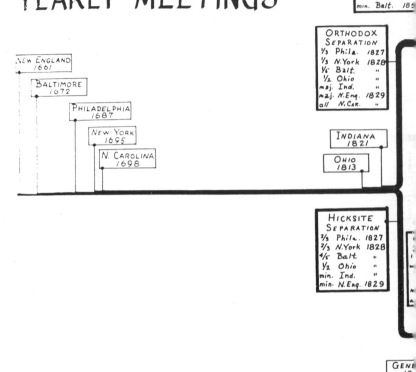

WILBURITE SEPARATION
1/14 N. Eng. 18–
min. N.York 18–
2/3 Ohio 185
Ind. "
min. Balt. 185

ORTHODOX SEPARATION
1/3 Phila. 1827
1/3 N.York 1828
1/5 Balt. "
1/2 Ohio "
maj. Ind. "
maj. N.Eng. 1829
all N.Car. "

NEW ENGLAND
1661

BALTIMORE
1672

PHILADELPHIA
1687

NEW YORK
1695

N. CAROLINA
1698

INDIANA
1821

OHIO
1813

HICKSITE SEPARATION
2/3 Phila. 1827
2/3 N.York 1828
4/5 Balt. "
1/2 Ohio "
min. Ind. "
min. N.Eng. 1829

GENE
18

155   1680   1700   1720   1740   1760   1780   1800   1820

FIRST AMERICAN YEARLY
MEETINGS ESTABLISHED

SEPAR

Reproduced from *Quakers on the Am*
Courtesy of Friends United Press